Down and Out In Padstow and London

By Alex Watts

"Reading 'Down and Out in Padstow and London' is a serious test for any food writer. Not only has Alex Watts done what all of us say we would like to do, tested his mettle in a professional kitchen, he also writes about his experiences so well that you spend as much time being jealous of his writing skills as you do of his experiences. It's an annoyingly enjoyable read."

- Simon Majumdar, author of two food/travel memoirs, Eat My Globe and Eating For Britain

* * * ~ ~ ~ * * *

Down and Out In Padstow and London

By Alex Watts

Copyright 2012 Alex Watts

Published by Completely Novel

* * * ~ ~ ~ * * *

Contents

*Dedicated to my mother and father,
Jenny and Brian Watts,
and to my good friend
Dom Bailey*

CHAPTER ONE

A few years ago, something strange happened to me – I decided to give everything up and retrain as a chef. I had a fairly interesting job – I worked as a journalist in London, and the money and hours weren't too bad either. But I was too comfortable – I needed to kick off the slippers and feel alive again.

Of course, I didn't go into it completely blind. I knew professional cooking was hard – the long hours, bad pay, bollockings and hurled pots. But I didn't know how much of it was true. And maybe that was partly it? Maybe in some sort of deluded manner I wanted to prove myself, and find salvation through suffering? Perhaps it was like the SAS – and I could prove I was a man by crawling on my hands and knees across Dartmoor?

The cheffing idea had been hanging around like a bad smell for years; a mad urge that I could never quite shake off. I'd always loved tinkering in the kitchen, reading cookbooks and trying out recipes, but that had never really been enough. I felt that unless I finally gave it a go and threw myself into the cramped furnace, I'd never be able to rest.

You see, I wanted to find out how the professionals do it. I wanted the blurred-action knife skills you see on TV. I wanted to learn from the best, and one day own a fish restaurant overlooking the sea. Nothing fancy – just a glimpse of the harbour would do. But most of all, I wanted to do something with my life. Be the one being interviewed, not the one scribbling into a note pad - the flame, not the fat moth wheezing round it.

It was a big ask, whichever way you looked at it. I'd only worked in a professional kitchen once in my life. It was after university, in between working at a garden centre and deciding to become a poet. A wind-blown corpse of a pub, so empty it made a buffet bar at a lepers' colony look busy. The customers looked like extras from Deliverance – web-footed types that play the banjo, and boast how their father is the best kisser in the village.

It started fairly well, but I got sacked on the second night for burning a saucepan full of rice. The landlord couldn't cook either – but compared to me he was Marie-Antoine Careme himself. It was a painful lesson. The world is filled with passionate foodies able to quote chunks of Larousse Gastronomique, but put them in a professional kitchen, and they are as useful as a snooze button on a smoke alarm.

That was why I wasn't going to be one of those over-confident fools who think they can run a restaurant with little or no experience. That was why I'd start at the bottom, getting my arse kicked around all day as a commis chef (the lowest rank in the kitchen, and a term freely interchangeable with slave, grunt, and dog's body.) After all, it would only be for a year or two. Wouldn't it?

I handed in my notice and went freelance at the paper. I figured I could just about survive on three news shifts a week, which would give me two or three days to work in a professional kitchen somewhere. It was a slow start. I spent the first few days lounging around, watching re-runs of Keith Floyd on the telly, and wondering how the hell a 41-year-old man went about retraining as a chef. Then Harriet, who ran the showbiz desk, phoned. She was interviewing Rick Stein for a feature, and wanted help compiling a list of questions to ask him. I thought about it for a while, knowing she wouldn't like it, but asked anyway.

"Do you mind if I come along as well? I've always wanted to meet him..."

I was right - she wasn't keen.

2

"I thought you hated celebrity chefs!"

"Not Stein!"

He was one of the old school. Second only to Floyd in my book.

"Well only if you don't upset him, and only speak to him after I've interviewed him..."

She had become business-like all of a sudden. Gone was the fluffy exterior - you had to be tough in showbiz.

A few days later, I went along for the interview, and found myself in a swanky bar in Mayfair. Stein looked shaky and tired as though his blood had been replaced with salad cream.

"This is the acquaintance of mine I was telling you about," Harriet said after she'd finished the interview. "He wants to have a quick chat with you..."

I shook the TV chef's hand and began blurting out a load of nonsense. He took a step back, staring into the eyes of a madman.

"I've always been into cooking, and well...I love cooking fish...in fact, it's my favourite...and I just wanted to pick your brains about being...well, about being a chef..."

He told me he would have a quick chat afterwards. I waited for him to finish the rest of the interviews, and listened as he churned out the same anecdotes to each journalist.

Harriet came over at one point. "Don't be too pushy. I don't care because I'll never see him again. Just think of something specific you can ask him."

I stood there confused, wondering what the hell I was doing. I started babbling again.

3

"Well, why don't you ask him if you can do a week in his restaurant," she said.

I waited for an hour, and mid-way through Stein's PR woman slid up and tried her best to get rid of me. It was obvious she saw me as an unhinged interloper who'd do nothing to promote his new book.

"We've got a car arriving soon," she said finally, "so I don't know if Rick will have time to talk to you."

As the last camera crew began packing up, she muttered something to the celebrity chef, and pointed at her watch.

"No, I'll see him," Stein said, beckoning me over.

This time I knew exactly what to say. The confusion left his face immediately, and he agreed to let me do a week in his kitchen. He wrote my name down in a tatty notebook, warned me he was very forgetful, and said I should ring his PA if I hadn't heard anything in a couple of days.

I felt excited, terrified, and alive. I stood at the bar for a long time afterwards, glowing in the thought of what had taken place. Maybe my luck was finally changing? If it wasn't just talk, I was to spend a week in one of the most famous restaurants in Britain. Then I thought of something I'd long ago locked away. That clichéd moment in movies when they gaze up and remember a childhood memory...and it all goes soft-focused and hazy...

I could smell the salt again; feel the sun on my skin. I was five-years-old, running round rock-pools, bucket in hand, when I spotted a huge scallop gleaming like a pink, fiery beacon. I took it back to our tent and handed it to my mother. But she hadn't got a clue what to do with it, so she gave it to the French family next door.

They cooked it with bacon and other secrets, and served it to me in the shell. I think at that moment, as I sat there realising there were even more delicious things in life than Golden Nuggets, I decided to become a chef. But it was a long time ago, and it is funny how easy it is to get distracted.

Three decades later, I was about to start the pilgrimage I should have embarked on long ago– a gruelling journey filled with hardship, blisters and chafing. And in my drunken haze I thought that just as the scallop was the emblem of the pilgrims that walked to Santiago de Compostella, it would become mine too. Where they suffered blisters and aching feet, mine would be cuts, burns, long hours and extremely bad pay.

It was a splendid, romantic notion and I ordered another drink, keen not to let the booze-fuelled afternoon steel ooze away, and leave me with the nagging doubt that it was all a ridiculous idea, and I'd never do it.

STEIN WAS not as forgetful as I'd feared. His PA phoned the next day, and the following week I drove down the M4 for a week's work experience at his Seafood Restaurant in Padstow. I rented a small cottage within walking distance, and went on a tour of the local pubs to get a flavour of the town. Besides, I was nervous and thought a few beers would help.

Most of the locals rolled their eyes when I brought up the TV chef's name. I could see why they called it Padstein - he had four restaurants, staff houses, hotels, a deli, patisserie, gift shop and cookery school all crammed into a fishing village with a population of less than 4,000. You could hardly look in a shop window without seeing his face beaming back at you. There were Rick Stein tea towels, oven gloves, mugs, marmalade, chutneys, fudge, pickles, olive oil and spices.

He was even selling jars of salt for £3 each. His Cornish pasties alone had upset the locals, who were appalled at him using the 'wrong' pastry, let alone smoked haddock or crab for fillings.

"It's bloody Scaarwtch mist he's selling in them jars," one old boy said.

Apparently, Stein hated the name Padstein and would argue: "I've just got a few modest businesses – it's not like I own the whole town!"

The locals blamed him for driving up property prices – forcing their children to move from their families somewhere cheaper, where they might one day stand a chance of owning their own home.

The TV chef and his prop dog Chalky had certainly put the place on the map though. And I wasn't sure how much those old fishermen had grumbled when hordes of grockles and emmets descended, blocking up the lanes with their Chelsea tractors, and handing over £250,000 and more for tiny weekend retreat cottages. I bet they couldn't stop rubbing their barnacled hands with glee.

Some remembered Stein in the early days – and how he hadn't always harboured ambitions of being a chef. The Seafood Restaurant had started out as a nightclub, and he'd gone into cooking when it was closed down by the police.

There were tales of his legendary tempers in the kitchen. Even his old friends described him as "very volatile in the early days" and "pretty fiery and stressed out". Stein, himself, admits he was "hot and bothered and fucking angry a lot of the time".

It was hard to reconcile that anger with the quiet, shy man I'd met in London. But then, by his own admittance, he'd mellowed significantly over the years. The books, TV deals, vineyard and house in Australia, meant that like most celebrity

6

chefs he rarely ventured into the kitchen to do the job that had made him famous.

As with Gordon Ramsay and Heston Blumenthal et al, he had trained up a team of staff so he could leave behind the heat and exhaustion of the stove for the cosy media world. It was strange to think I was doing it in reverse. I was clearly insane, but then, apparently, you had to be mad to be a good chef.

An old waitress, who had been there in the early days, said deep down Stein was a shy man. It reminded me of his words in a documentary I'd seen: "I always seem to be quite lively and enjoying myself, but actually I'm taking pleasure in my food and the fact people are enjoying it. I'm not making a big fuss about it. I think that's the core of what being a restaurateur is all about - actually taking pleasure in other people's happiness."

I admired him for that, and his philosophy that "nothing is more joyful or exhilarating than fresh fish simply cooked". It was what thrilled me about cooking too; it was that sort of cheffing I wanted to learn. Brilliant, fresh ingredients cooked in a simple manner. There's nothing worse than Britain's scourge of gastropubs and uber-trendy restaurants boasting pretentious monstrosities like salmon candyfloss, almond fluid gels, and lavender jus. What's wrong with steak and kidney pudding and pea and ham soup?

The waitress told me that when Stein opened the restaurant in 1975, the dishes were really simple: sea bass and samphire with beurre blanc, mackerel with dill and new potatoes, clam chowder with razor clams from the Camel estuary, moules marinieres, skate with black butter, and that yardstick of all good seafood restaurants - fish soup.

He won awards, but he didn't hit the big time until Keith Floyd became a regular visitor, and convinced his director David Pritchard to include Stein in one of his Floyd On Fish programmes. After that the phone didn't stop ringing, and even well-dressed lobsters had to book. Floyd showed him how to make a good bouillabaisse, and now I was going to learn those skills myself. I went to bed proud and extremely nervous.

I walked down the hill and looked out at the fishing boats in the harbour. It was worth going to work just for the view. The salty air was filled with the screams of gulls, and I thought of Dylan Thomas and Captain Cat. Far out in the bay, a fishing vessel was heading home, surrounded by what looked like tiny scraps of white tissue paper. For some reason, it reminded me of Eric Cantona's famous quote: "When the seagulls follow the trawler, it is because they think sardines will be thrown into the sea."

I had a final cigarette, and walked round the harbour to the restaurant, past the spot where they filmed Stein eating roast bass on a trawler with Floyd as they sailed off to sea. Dinner jackets, a starched linen tablecloth, and silverware knives and forks. It was the spirit of adventure in Floyd's programmes that had attracted Stein to the TV world. I wondered what fish I'd get by following Stein's trawler. But then, I thought, as I walked up to the door – the sea hath fish for every man.

I TOOK a deep breath and walked in, wondering what the hell lay ahead. I gave my name at reception, and was told to wait in the conservatory area for the head chef to arrive. I sat there among the plants, flicking through a menu.

It was true what they said about Stein putting chilli in everything. He couldn't leave the stuff alone. There was monkfish vindaloo; Goan lobster curry; Singapore chilli crab; hot shellfish platter with chilli; smoked mackerel and green mango salad with bird eye chillies; mussels, clams and cockles masala; and grilled scallops with chilli and coriander sauce.

8

I was about to check whether there was any chilli in the desserts when Raymond the head chef rushed in, and apologised for making me wait. I was surprised by the fuss - the last time I'd done any work experience, they'd asked for tea every two seconds, and sent me out to buy a tin of striped paint.

I'd been convinced that despite my age, the same was going to happen at the restaurant. I thought when they weren't asking me to dice flour and wash salt, they'd be yelling at me to fetch strawberry deseeders, left-handed parsley curlers, and cans of mise-en-place.

It soon became obvious that Raymond wasn't sure how good a friend I was of Stein's, and was taking no chances. He led me through the restaurant and introduced me to the staff. The kitchen was light and airy and there was no smell of fish. The white-tiled walls gleamed under the fluorescent lights. In the centre was a large stove area, with stockpots and bubbling saucepans. One of the chefs handed me a freshly-boiled langoustine. It was delicious.

The forelock-tugging continued as Raymond showed me each section of the kitchen, and then it stopped suddenly when I was introduced to a stocky man with cropped hair called Ted the Turbot. He looked me up and down as if choosing a ragworm for a hook, and pointed at the pass.

"There's the coffee machine, I take two sugars," he growled.

The chefs were preparing for lunch service, and I was put on starters with a cook called Daniel. He took an immediate dislike to me for some reason. After he'd discovered I couldn't even cut herbs straight, let alone prep tomato concasse or the other more complicated garnishes, he must have had a word with Raymond because after breakfast I was transferred to the veg section.

9

I worked with Dave, a 17-year-old commis chef, cutting up boxes of veg. He handed me a razor-sharp Global blade, and was alarmed at my knife skills - no claw, just clumsy, out-stretched fingers. He told me about a lad who had gone for a trial there and was so nervous he'd cut off a finger, and that made me feel even more useless and anxious.

Raymond came over at one point and said I'd be spending the next day at Stein's Cornish pasty unit to "give me a taste of the whole operation". He said they started early, and I'd need to be up there at 6am. It was on an industrial estate a couple of miles from Padstow, and Dave drove me up there in the afternoon split between our shifts to show me where it was.

I was then moved to Ted the Turbot's section, near the ice machines at the foot of the stairs. He didn't get me to do any work - he could see there was no point. I just stood there watching him filleting mackerel. He said he'd spent most of his life working as a fishmonger. I'd never seen a chef with better knife skills.

Four swift turns, and a second later two baby-smooth fillets lay on the counter. He looked like he could do it in his sleep. Blade up the back and along the backbone, follow it along, head off, and within minutes there was a row of prepped fish. One fillet lay on the marble slab, the other hung off the edge, joined by the tail.

He got out a tub of red paste, dipped a teaspoon in, and smeared it over the flesh, before pushing the fillets together. He tied them with string, three loops in perfect symmetry. It was a depressing reminder of how much I had to learn.

I stood there watching Ted for the rest of the afternoon, vainly trying to remember each knife stroke. He ignored most of my questions.

"You've done that before," I said in a final effort.

"Once or twice," he replied.

There was silence again for another 20 minutes.

"So what goes in the red paste?"

"I don't know - I'm not a chef, just a fishmonger..."

Then a glint came into his eyes.

"Try it..."

He handed me a heaped spoon. The fiery paste incinerated my tongue and left scorch-marks on my gums. It was an hour before my tongue recovered. He warmed up a bit after that.

"Sounds weird chilli masala and mackerel, doesn't it. But it works," he said. "And these are the best part of a tenner each - from a 50p fish!"

He was clearly impressed by the mark-up. A few pence of spices, a few flourishes from a skilled chef, and you had a profit margin that would make a banker blush. The dish was called mackerel recheado, and Stein had got it from Goa, where it was served with freshly-made naan bread.

There was more silence, and I had another stab at conversation.

"What about all the trimmings? Do you use them for stock?"

Ted stopped what he was doing, put his knife down, and frowned at me as though I was a village idiot who'd just wandered in with a pasty in my hand.

"They're oily fish! They're no good for stock!"

Then I watched him prep the rest of the fish. The Dover soles had dark little eyes that seemed to watch each knife stroke mournfully. A flash of steel behind its tiny head, and the guts

11

were gone, and then scissors to remove the spines round the edge. For service, they were rubbed hard with a cloth until they were as dry as a bone, then brushed with a thick green thyme oil and chargrilled.

When one of the soles was left for too long under the lights, Raymond handed it to me. It was deliciously moist and full of flavour - the same sweet-nut, autumnal taste as the harbour air.

That night as I walked to my bed, I was on a high. I hadn't actually done anything, but just by being there I felt part of the action. I was still basking in the good feeling, looking at the lights from the fishing boats and thinking about the next day's pasties, when it all went horribly wrong.

I'd planned to have an early night, get up at 5am, and drive up to the industrial unit for a day learning about side-crimping. But Colin, a photographer I knew from the paper, rang to say he was in a pub overlooking the harbour and had got me a drink in. He was doing a piece on the 'snob yobs' that pillage Rock – one of Prince William's favourite haunts. I promised myself it would only be one or two and walked back down the hill.

Colin was fishing cockles from a jar. He looked like he'd been there some time. He wanted to hear all about my new career, and kept running off to refill our glasses. At some point, I crawled up the hill to my room. I was too drunk to remember my alarm, and woke at nine with a stinking headache.

I don't know what happened, but still drunk, and embarrassed by the thought of going in late, I found myself agreeing to go on a fishing trip with Colin. I was braving my first cigarette of the day when Raymond phoned. He sounded confused, and slightly hurt.

"I just wanted to know you were alright," he explained, almost apologetically.

My head was still thumping, and I babbled about my friend coming down and how I'd promised him a fishing trip. A few minutes past, and Stein's executive chef Jimmy phoned. He was far more direct.

"Why dinnae you dae the pasties this morning Lennie?"

I was unnerved by the change in tone. It was in stark contrast to Raymond's brown-nosing. I muttered something about being out late and waking up with a hangover, hoping he'd understand. At the time, I didn't realise how pathetic that would sound to a chef.

"Oh, mibbe ah goat it wrong," he said, "Rick dinnae say much abit you – ah thought you waur here tae learn!"

"I am..." I said.

I tried to make light of it, and then thought of something and wished I hadn't.

"If I catch some fish...I'll bring them to the restaurant..."

My sentence trailed off into a dark silence.

"Awright, yir gaun tae seel them to us?"

I felt terrible. I'd been given a brilliant opportunity to learn, and all I'd done was thrown it back in their faces. No wonder they were pissed off. Looking back on it, I still don't know why I went out on that boat.

I walked back into the restaurant that afternoon, and after changing into my whites, was summoned to Jimmy's office. He was there with one of the managers.

"Sae whit happened the-day whit the pasties?"

13

I began jabbering again, apologising profusely, and moaning about how I hadn't brought an alarm clock. They made me squirm for a bit, then asked why I hadn't used the alarm on my mobile phone.

I was forced to make more pathetic excuses. It must have been painful to watch. I promised them I wanted to learn as much as possible, and vainly hoped that would be the end of the matter. But Jimmy was enjoying himself.

"Sae whit exactly dae ye dae?"

"I'm retraining as a chef. I gave up my job as a journalist..."

The word slipped out before I could stop it. The manager began eyeing me suspiciously. She was one of those scary, orange-skinned public school girl types.

"Do you still write anything?" she asked.

"No, not really," I lied.

"Not really?"

"Sae yoo're nae haur tae dae a hatchit job oan us 'en?" Jimmy said. "Coz ah would be pished off if ye waur..."

I assured him I wasn't, and then he came at me again. The Glaswegian accent scared me at the best of times.

"Sae who was that bloke wi' ye – that one wi' th' camera?"

I wondered how he knew about Colin. Then I realised Stein's people must have spies everywhere. After all, he did own half the town.

"Oh, just a friend...he's a twitcher. He's down here looking for the, err, Elder Flycatcher...one's been spotted near here apparently..."

14

I thought it best not to tell them Colin was a pap for a Sunday red-top. They let me go, and managed a pair of weak smiles. I was about to walk off when Jimmy called me back.

"We won't say anythin' tae Rick thes time. I'll teel the boys yoo're awright, an' yoo're haur tae learn."

"Thanks chef," I said.

I walked down the stairs into the furnace, still reeling from the interrogation. The first chef I met was the sour Belgian who filled in for Ted on his days off.

"How's your hangover?" he sneered.

I had no idea at the time my absence would carry such news. As I know now, there are no secrets in a kitchen, and even the tiniest piece of gossip is seized upon. In fact, given the long hours, and so many people crammed between four walls, secrets spread like foot and mouth.

After more harsh looks, I walked over to Dave, the youngster who'd given me a lift to the pasty unit. I stuffed a tenner in his hand for the petrol, and apologised.

"It's alright – If I wasn't being paid, I wouldn't have got up either," he shrugged. But I could sense his hurt.

We were setting up for the evening, and I'd kept my head down, and thought I'd got over the worst of it, when a waitress cornered me. She said her boyfriend ran the pasty unit, and had spent the whole of the previous night planning my day.

"We were supposed to be going round my parents' house for a meal," she whined, "but Tommy said he was too busy..." Her voice was like a knife that had been stuck in a lemon too long.

15

At the end of the evening, I felt weary and chastened, like the pilgrims who follow the scallop shells to Santiago de Compostela. I vowed to work as hard as I could for the rest of the week whatever they chucked at me.

THE NEXT day I was chopping onions when Stein walked in. He crept up behind the sous chef, tapped him on the shoulder, and eyeballed the dishes going out from the pass. The cocky bravado left the Italian instantly. I hoped to God that Stein hadn't found out about the pasties.

It seemed odd, but on the outside – in the media world - Stein appeared a very nervous, twitchy figure. But he grew into a bear as he entered his former lair. He frowned a few times, almost sniffing the air, as he scanned the kitchen. Then his eyes fell on me, and he squinted. He said something to the fawning Italian and pointed.

From the look on his face, I was sure he knew about the pasties. I kept my head down and carried on chopping. Long minutes past as Stein worked his way through the kitchen. He walked past the stove area, looked in at the pastry section, and I was praying he was going to carry on through the fish prep area and disappear up the stairs, when he strolled towards me.

I sped up the chopping in a pointless attempt to make it look like I knew what I was doing. I got a glimpse of his shadow and then he was upon me.

"So how are you finding it?" he said. "Hard work?"

I looked up pretending to see him for the first time, and gave him my best grin. All I could think about was those fucking pasties.

"Oh, it's fantastic!" I said. "I'm learning a huge amount. You know, I really appreciate the chance you've given me..."

We chatted for a few more seconds, but I couldn't think of what to say, so I asked him what he was doing the next day.

"I'm flying to Australia...as you do. Anyway good luck with it, and I'm glad you managed to arrange the week so, er, quickly."

He let the sentence float in mid-air, and I knew it wasn't just Jimmy and the manager who were worried I might be doing a hatchet job.

That evening I ditched the booze and had an early night, determined to be fresh in the morning. But when I walked in, Raymond took me to one side and bollocked me for not shaving. Something had changed in his attitude, and it wasn't anything good. I wasn't sure if it was just the pasties. He told me to go out and buy a razor, and to come back when I was clean-shaven.

I trawled through the fishing village, but all they had was fudge, postcards and pasties. Eventually I found a corner shop selling those single-blade efforts women use on their legs. I shaved in the staff changing room, cutting myself several times as I hacked away. I had to wait five minutes for the bleeding to stop.

"That's better," Raymond said, looking at the clods of tissue stuck to my face. He stared at me for a few seconds, as though seeing me for the first time.

"I heard about Rick coming into the kitchen last night..." He mimicked a squint and cupped his brow with his hand as though shielding his eyes from the sun. "'Who's that?' he said...maybe...maybe it was the hat, he didn't recognise you..."

My cover was blown. He knew I wasn't a business associate of Stein's at all, or worse, a relative. The protection I'd been afforded by the possibility evaporated in an instant. And there were still the pasties to consider...

From that moment on, he threw all the worst jobs at me and treated me like any other galley slave. Up to that point, I'd had no idea how much tedious manual labour goes into expensive restaurant food, but I soon found out.

The parsley alone took me hours. I went through bags of the stuff, picking leaf from stalk, and chopping it into green dust. It was a far cry from dinner party cooking, and all that recipe book guff.

I had to plough through boxes of cavolo nero (or black kale as it is known outside of expensive restaurants in Cornwall). Whenever I asked if there was enough, they replied: "Well it's all got to be done..." After stripping out the central stalk and rolling then slicing the good stuff, I blanched the greens for a minute in boiling water, and then refreshed them in iced water to stop the colour fading. Then, when an order came in, the strips were pan-fried in oil and butter with fennel seeds and finely sliced garlic.

Stein seemed to use garlic almost as much as he used chilli, and I was given hundreds of bulbs to prep. You had to peel each clove, without crushing it, and slice it so finely it almost dissolved in the oil. After that I moved on to the croutons for the fish soup. Each slice of French bread was fried until golden in sunflower oil, and then handed to me to rub both sides with a halved clove of garlic. None of the tasks were complicated enough to trouble a slug, but there was no point in giving me anything more tricky, and besides, I didn't deserve it.

Another job was picking through the shrimps, which were boiled and served with freshly-made mayonnaise on the bar menu. You had to painstakingly filter through buckets of ocean floor to get a few hundred. God knows who brought them in – maybe Neptune himself. Seaweed, pebbles, anemones, small fish, crabs and all manner of debris were mixed in with those tiny morsels. The shrimps without heads, or the ones that looked bad, were thrown. After a few thousand, my fingers would ache, but there was always another bucket to tackle.

But the worst chore of all was chopping vanilla pods for the sea bass sauce. Without decent knife skills, it took me far longer than it should have done, and soon I had developed a nasty blister on the palm of my right hand. I had to halve each pod, and carefully scrape out the vanilla seeds, and then chop the husks finely. It was like trying to cut leather with a spoon. I'd spend an hour doing just ten, the blade see-sawing away, and the knife handle and sweat burning my blister.

Every time I checked with Raymond, he told me it had to be finer. Eventually, when the black dust was as fine as sieved flour, they took it away and reduced it with three litres of fish stock and peeled shallots until there were just a few thimbles of black treacle in memory of my hard work.

And when I wasn't chopping vanilla, or prepping shrimps, or running to the dry store, or de-seeding tomatoes, I was told to pick chervil. Bags of the stuff.

I went about my work quietly, looking over from time to time at the jet-trails of white as the chefs did service. You could smell the adrenaline in the greasy, pungent air, and that more than anything made me want to be a chef. I looked at them enviously with their flame-grilled faces; juggling orders in a frenzied haze, hot pans spitting like trapped cobras, rocking on their heels like boxers, pirouetting past each other to the yell of 'BACKS!' It was like watching a runaway train screaming into a bend, rattling and swaying and ready to explode.

That was why chefs put up with the poor pay and long hours, I thought. Those precious moments of white-knuckle service. Fuck the office job. Fuck working for the man. Fuck being passed over for promotion.

The only trouble was there were a few hundred wheelbarrows of chervil between me and the grill, and one day running my own restaurant. The path would be long and arduous. I had no doubt about that. You only had to look at their faces. But then, as an Irish friend who'd also gone into cheffing late in life liked to say: "You need an old dog for the hard road."

Some of them clearly saw themselves as kitchen warriors, showing off their scars and fighting each day like it was their last. They missed the 150-plus covers of the summer, when the air conditioning had stopped working, pushing the temperature in the kitchen past 50C.

"Just 100 in tonight," one chef moaned before service. "It'll be a quiet night."

Then as we were clearing down...

"It wasn't a bad night, only 93, but they all came at the same time."

"Yeah, we got hit well tonight," agreed an Aussie.

Cooking was so different from office work. Offices were filled with clock-watchers, ready to grab their coats and sprint out the door the moment the small hand hit five. But for a chef, there was never enough time in the day. And when it was over and the cleaning done, they basked in the glories like fighters discussing a battle. It was something missing from office life. Management gurus might talk about the need for team-building through away days and survival courses, but once you've learned how to build a raft, you return an unhappy, spineless backstabber again.

The chefs might have been ready to rip out each other's throats in the heat of service - "Why the fuck are you asking him to sort the meat out? He's on starters! Put the fucking veal bones in the milk yourself!" began one argument - but afterwards, the insults were quickly forgotten. And after a couple of days toiling like a devil, I felt part of it too.

I burned a naan bread moments before the monkfish vindaloo went out, and tried to blame it on my eyesight, only to come under a storm of derision and threats on my life. But afterwards, they just laughed and muttered something about everyone making mistakes. Only the female Kiwi chef who'd had to make another naan in lightning speed was still pissed off.

"Jeez, I don't know how you can burn it if you're stood there like a twat watching it under the grill!"

During one rare chatty moment, Ted the Turbot told me that if he was in power, he'd make all school-leavers wash pots for a year – just to give them "a sense of perspective". He said kitchens make you work hard and appreciate even the pettiest of life's pleasures. I reckoned there might have been something in that. Sleep, alone, as Orwell pointed out, is a magical experience when you've been sweating all day in a cramped furnace.

On my last day, I was sent to Stein's cookery school overlooking the harbour. There was a curious mixture of wealthy foodies, some hoping to learn enough to open their own restaurant. They really thought it was that simple. Occasionally, one would speak into a Dictaphone: "Chef says put the skate wing in the boiling stock and then switch off the gas and let it cook through."

They would probably go the way of the thousands of untrained no-hopers before them, who had quickly learned that being able to host a successful dinner party is no preparation for running a professional kitchen. That was why I wanted to do it the hard way.

That evening, I went back to my menial tasks at the restaurant, and finished the week with a glowing accolade. It happened as I was blanching leeks. Daniel was looking over from the starter section.

"Chef, can we have some more parsley?"

I looked behind me, then realised he was talking to me. It was the first time in my life I'd been called 'chef' and I can't tell you how proud I was.

I said my goodbyes, bought Raymond a bottle of expensive claret, which he didn't seem too impressed with, and drove back up the M4, my heart full of pride. For the first time in years, the indecision was gone. I knew I wanted to be a chef, and run my own restaurant. I just didn't know how I was going to do it.

CHAPTER TWO

After a couple of days back at the paper, the drudgery took over, and that week in Padstein seemed a long way away. Soon my world had shrunk to a few late-night bars. There was no sorcery to sleep anymore, no magical softness to the sheets, just a few grey hours until dawn.

I was desperate to get back in the kitchen, so I phoned Raymond for a job. He said it was the low season, and anyway I needed an NVQ. I could tell he was trying to fob me off. The thought of spending a year or two in college with spotty 16-year-olds horrified me.

I looked at the various cordon bleu cooking schools in London. But they seemed to be the preserve of bored housewives, who wanted to impress their husband's clients by boning their own ducks. One of the young chefs at Stein's had done a six-month course in London that had cost his parents £10,000. He said he'd learned more in his first month at the fish restaurant.

Like him, I knew the only way to get good was to get experience in a professional kitchen. But I also knew I would need a reasonable knowledge of the college repertoire: turning potatoes into six-sided barrels, sauce Veronique and Espagnole, creme anglais, souffles, that sort of thing. I bought an NVQ2 food preparation course book and worked my way through it in the evenings, trying out techniques and recipes. I also practised my knife skills, chopping bags of onions until the blade felt like an extension of my arm.

One night, I turned on the TV, and there was John Torode and his egg-headed pal Greg 'the Veg' Wallace. They were hovering around a pretty 23-year-old Masterchef contestant sporting a low cut top. The breathy voiceover described her as "an inventive cook who loves making exciting new dishes". She was making a cheese and smoked haddock tart.

Egg was poking his nose in, with all the smugness and grace of a taxi driver who'd just won the lottery. He was dressed from head to toe in black Armani.

"Is it cooking?" he drooled. "Is it going to be ready in six minutes?"

"Maybe."

"Maybe not," said Toad, "because the oven's not on."

"You're joking – oh my God," she squealed.

"Now the pressure's on," leered Egg.

Even I could do better than that, I thought. There was only one thing for it. I fired up my lap-top and applied to go on Masterchef. I sat there looking at the questions on the online form. I had no idea what to put down.

The whole show was a farce. The prize was a job as a trainee chef at a top London restaurant. They didn't say how much you'd get, or what the hours were, or what to do when you're thrown out on the street because you can't pay the rent.

Maybe the prize didn't exist at all. I mean, who the hell would take them up on it? The whole thing was about getting on the telly, and society's mushrooming obsession with fame. I couldn't see any of the contestants swapping their cushy jobs for 16 hours a day of back-breaking toil on a wage just enough to keep them alive. Not if there weren't any cameras about anyway.

The recent winners and finalists seemed to be too busy churning out recipe books and opening fetes to spend much time actually learning the trade. All I knew was that even if I did get in the finals, it was unlikely to lead to any proper paid cooking work. I needed professional training and a way to support myself if I was to do it properly.

There was also the time delay. The programme was likely to be months away, and I was dying to get back in the kitchen. One hopeful had to wait eight months before the producers contacted him, then spent 40 minutes on the phone whispering about why he wanted to be a chef with his boss earwigging in the background.

What the hell. I filled in the form anyway...

'Why do you enjoy cooking?' It was a good question. Usually you save the toughest for last. Well you do in journalism anyway – that way it doesn't matter if they walk out. What they wanted, I figured, was some sort of epiphany moment or anecdotal nugget that might make a mention on the show.

'I've always loved food and cooking, ever since I found a scallop on a beach while on holiday in France, around the age of five, and a French family in the next tent cooked it for me,' I began.

'Who is your favourite chef?' You probably think you can guess what I put. No, not Floyd. Torode. Yes, I know. You can't stand the dreadful man either - the way he crams great forkfuls of food into his gob while mumbling. But I knew a little toadying wouldn't hurt. And as a journalist, I knew all about that.

'List three ingredients that you could not live without.' I thought about putting air, food and water, then just put coriander, garlic and chilli.

The next was how long I'd been cooking for. What did they mean? Proper cooking or first gingerbread moment? I went for first gingerbread moment. 'From the age of five – about 36 years.'

Then it was the food I liked. I'd read somewhere that Egg hated contestants spouting out clichés like "rustic charm" and "simple, locally-sourced ingredients". Giving a glimmer of his enormous talent, and scotching any suspicions that he was just a grocer who had been in the right place at the right time, he liked to reply: "So tell me what a complex local ingredient might be..."

How would you cope with that? The man was clearly destined for bigger things than Masterchef. Perhaps Question Time beckoned?

'What is your greatest ambition in life?' I was about to put 'to run a seafront restaurant– nothing flash, just a glimpse of the harbour would do' when I remembered how Egg hated "restaurant by the sea" clichés as well, so for some reason I typed "head chef at a mountain resort".

'What is the hardest cooking situation you have ever been in?' I knew they'd have a skewed perception of that. When the programme starts, Egg and Toad explain they're looking for "a great amateur cook who can make it as a professional." Svengalis selling the notion that cheffing offers some sort of idyllic paradise far removed from the soulless drudgery of the contestants' daily lives.

In one show, a small, dumpy clerk tells Toad why she wants to be a chef. "As much as I love my job, I find it emotionally draining, and I find cooking very relaxing," she says. "How fab would that be to do that, and get paid for it as your job?"

You could only admire the hope. She, like me, just wanted happiness. She concentrated on the dream, not the thought of getting abused and kicked round a kitchen all day, under a ceaseless barrage of insults and orders: "Get on with the spuds! Watch those bloody apples don't catch! Chop those fucking carrots! How long for that risotto? 30 seconds chef! You've got 20! What's black and lives in the oven?"

26

Next there is a shot of a professional chef in action – he's shaking a frying pan, the very flames of Hades flashing in the lens. He rattles the mussels again, liquor spills, and more flames shoot up and engulf the pan. Then it cuts to someone squeezing herb oil round a plate. They're taking ages, so it must be one of the contestants.

Cut to the Egg...

"Cooking doesn't get tougher than this," he boasts, puffing out his moobs like a camp wrestler. "It's difficult, it should be difficult – this is Masterchef." His voice rises dramatically at the end as if suddenly possessed by the spirit of a man in tights.

"What the hell are you going on about?" I could imagine thousands of hairy-arsed chefs screaming at the telly, can in one hand, joint in the other. "Cooking gets a lot tougher than that, you bald twat!"

Inventing and cooking a dish in 50 minutes from a list of ingredients, serving up a two-course meal, and the so-called Pressure Test of doing lunch service in a publicity-hungry restaurant when you only have to deal with one dish! A fucking stroll in the park, they're thinking.

There was no mention of the brandings and humiliating initiation ceremonies. No mention of the weariness and high suicide rates. Just TV gloss. The true kitchen warriors could tell you tales about chefs being forced to stand in the corridor all night with their bollocks hanging out, telling every waitress who went past that they had a small penis.

In fact, they'd be only too happy to fill you in at great length on how "making it as a professional" as Toad puts it, can mean starting work at 8am each day, working until 2am, almost without a break, getting four hours sleep, and then doing it all again.

I finished off the last question. It was about my greatest achievement in life so far. I thought for a bit, then just put down the truth. "Spending a week in Rick Stein's restaurant...On the last day one of them called me chef – it doesn't sound much, but it gave me a real glow inside. I really felt I'd achieved something...'

There seemed to be enough arse-licking, celebrity chef endorsement, anecdotal nuggets, and outright lies to at least get me through to the regional heats. After that, I'd have to rely on my cooking skills and secretly practising the same two dishes every night like the other contestants.

I emailed the application form, with a photo as instructed. A day or so later I got a call from a researcher at Masterchef – young woman's voice, quite posh. I rubbed my eyes, and cleared my throat, trying to make it sound like I hadn't just woken up.

"So, Lennie, tell me about your passion for cooking," she began.

She asked me pretty much the same questions I'd filled in on the form. I tried to remember what I'd written, and cursed myself for not printing it out. The more I listened, the more I realised it was all a con. From her voice, she genuinely seemed to think Masterchef was offering people a chance to "embark on an absolute, life-changing journey".

There were no details about the prize cooking job, just lots about what sort of contestants they were looking for. She wanted to know whether I'd worked full-time as a professional chef before, if I had received an NVQ catering qualification or similar in the past ten years, and whether I had the required level of enthusiasm, drive, love of food, and desire, to change my life.

At one point, she asked if I had ever been convicted of a "serious crime". I thought that was a bit rich given Egg's conviction for football hooliganism over a youthful misdemeanour, but maybe it didn't include the presenters.

I began drifting off, thinking about the future. She had the same mee-jar voice as the show's narrator...

After 15 years in prison, Lennie is desperate for a life in food. In his heat, he blew the judges away with his chicken vindaloo.

"I'll quite happily stick my face in it," says Egg.

But sometimes he gives himself too much to do, and more often than not, it tastes better than it looks...

The cow, I thought. Then I wondered whether I'd said the word out loud. But the researcher was still talking.

"So the next stage is a casting day," she gushed. "You may get invited along for that, we don't know yet. We'll be interviewing about 8,000 people across the country and only choose 100 for the show..."

I had a one in 80 chance. I needed to get a proper cooking job.

I PASSED a catering agency advertising cooking jobs for £6 an hour. They didn't ask whether I had any experience. Once I'd filled out a few forms, a fat dwarf with a goatee threw a few questions at me. The interview was over in seconds.

"How do you make a béchamel sauce?" he asked.

"First you infuse the milk..."

"Infuse?"

"Yeah, boil the milk with bay leaves, peppercorns, and you can use an onion..."

29

His chubby fingers waved me on irritably.

"Then melt some butter in a pan, stir in some flour to make a roux...then slowly whisk in..."

"Yeah, yeah fine."

All he wanted to know was whether I knew how to make lasagne.

He phoned the next morning, but I was in bed after a night shift at the paper. By the time I phoned back, the job was gone. But I didn't want to work as a dinner lady anyway.

As I waited to hear about my Masterchef application, I began watching more and more episodes of the show - and it led to such an excruciatingly bad case of food poisoning, it felt like I'd been taken out for sushi by the KGB.

It began one Friday night, when I cooked a pork chop after coming back from the pub, and lasted a good five days. I didn't in any way blame my drunkenness; the blame lay solely at the door of those two rotten buggers, Egg and Toad.

Earlier that night, I'd watched a contestant serve up what could only be described as semi-cooked pork. Pink juice was oozing out, surrounding the parsnip mash.

Egg rams a generous forkful of pork, watercress and caramelised apple into his mouth, and looks thoughtful.

"What I get is that almost cider sweetness of that apple against the soft pork," he says. "I want a little bit more than that."

What like salmonella?

Toad dislocates his jaw like an Australian rock python devouring a sheep and takes an even bigger forkful. He half closes his hooded eyelids.

"It is really beautifully soft, well-cooked pork..."

Well-cooked? The thing was still twitching.

I hadn't bothered with the apples and mash, but I did have some wilted watercress in the fridge. And the homage to that great Masterchef dish was complete when I thought 'that'll do' and chucked it on a plate. I stabbed the soft pork, and pink juice oozed out beautifully.

"That's alright, perfectly cooked," I thought, remembering Toad's words.

The juice formed a nice gravy, and I mopped it up with bread. I can barely bring myself to think about what followed. My suffering would have been far less if I'd known Egg and Toad had, like me, spent the next week hurling like bulimic Romans, but somehow I knew they hadn't. So what the hell was the difference between my rare piece of pork and the one they had stuffed so enthusiastically into their gobs?

Round and round the question went as I spent five days flat on my arse. It made me have serious doubts about my cooking skills and my decision to retrain as a chef. If I'd served that in a restaurant in Eastbourne, I'd have killed a dozen pensioners. They'd have called me the Harold Shipman of the catering trade.

During the worst stages of the poisoning, I thought about my own epitaph...

"Here lies Lennie Nash. He followed his heart. PS. I told you that pork wasn't cooked."

As my gloom continued, I kept reflecting on my ridiculous decision to take up the knives at the age of 41 - more than two decades after most spotty-faced chefs do their training. Without the energy and resilience of youth, how could I survive long days in a hell-hole kitchen, my soul bleaching away under fluorescent lights?

And for what? So fat cat bankers could gorge themselves on gourmet food while boasting about their bonuses? Maybe undercooked pork wasn't such a bad idea after all, I thought as I said hello once again to the toilet.

A WEEK later I got an email from Masterchef, saying they were "very impressed" by my application. I was invited to a casting day at the Brunei Gallery in London. The letter said:

"Please bring along a sample of your cooking for our judges to taste. You only need to bring one dish. The team will be tasting lots of food so it does not need to be a big portion. It can be sweet or savoury and must be cold or something that can be eaten/tasted cold. We will take into account that the food is cold and has had to travel. Please note there are NO REHEATING FACILITIES and there will be minimal preparation time/facilities but you will have to plate and serve your dish.

"The auditions will be filmed for broadcast so we want you looking and feeling your best. Please avoid wearing white or cream, any logos and steer clear of thin stripes, small spots or geometric patterns. Remember we want your personality to shine through so make sure you feel happy and comfortable as possible....

"Due to the large number of applicants we will be unable to contact unsuccessful applicants."

I sat there thinking about what dish to go for, and wondering whether I had any clean shirts, let alone ones that weren't striped.

I knew it would have to be something that could sit happily in a humid Tube carriage half-way across London. So looking back on it now, I still don't know why I went for sushi. Or tuna tartare with cucumber and wasabi soup, as I called it. I'd seen it made in a restaurant somewhere and decided to copy it. It was easy to make, but it looked good. And, after all, as Egg and Toad liked to point out - you eat with your eyes.

You dice sashimi-grade, raw tuna and salmon, and do the same with an avocado. Then mix sesame oil, salt, pepper, lime juice and soy sauce in a bowl, and stir in the fish and avocado cubes. You leave it to marinade, and cut a peeled cucumber in half lengthways and remove the seeds by running a spoon down the middle. You blitz the chopped cucumber flesh with chicken stock, cream, wasabi, Worcester sauce and Tabasco, then strain the liquid and chill it.

You then plate the dish by putting an oiled chef's ring in the middle of a soup bowl, and fill it with layers of marinated salmon, tuna and avocado. You remove the ring, pour the chilled soup round the tartare, and garnish with a sprig of chervil and a few salmon eggs.

And that was the problem. I couldn't get salmon eggs anywhere in London. Every shop that did them had sold out. After a few hours of traipsing around delis and fishmongers, I realised I had about as much chance of getting my hands on a Dodo egg.

The last place I tried was a Japanese fishmonger called Atari-Ya hidden away in the suburbs of West Acton. They didn't have any salmon eggs either, so I settled for red and green tobiko (flying fish roe). I bought a chiller bag, and a thermos flask to carry the soup in, practised the dish a few times, and went to bed.

The Masterchef narrator's voice began...

After everything he's learned, can Lennie deliver a faultless dish? He's attempted a delicate combination of tuna tartare with a cucumber and wasabi soup...

33

Toad tucks in, destroying my beautiful tartare. He sniffs the raw fish before sticking it in his mouth.

"I think your flavours are good. You've got the rich oiliness of the fish; you've got the sweetness of the soup..."

Egg holds up a napkin to stop soup dripping down his Armani.

"That is deep! It's well seasoned - both the salmon and the tuna are cooked perfectly..."

What would I do? Tell him the fish was raw?

The alarm clock went off and I jumped out of bed.

Two hours later, I was outside the studios in Russell Square, smoking a cigarette. I spotted one of the contestants coming out after his audition. He was a fat man with a shaven head, and a smug grin. I asked him a few questions, but he wasn't giving anything away. This was Masterchef.

I lit another cigarette and texted a friend. I got one back saying: "Ur life's going to change in a massive way. This just the beginning!"

She got that right.

I had a last cigarette then walked in. I waited in the foyer with a couple of ladies from Dorset who'd brought in cakes. Why hadn't I made cakes? Raw fish was a dreadful idea. I thought about walking out and handing the stuff to the homeless. I could see the headline: "Masterchef Murderer Poisons Tramps".

Then I was called into a small room. Three judges were sitting on plastic chairs. There was no sign of Egg or Toad. Apparently, they didn't bother with the auditions. One of the three began filming as I took them through the dish.

You could tell they were reticent about eating raw fish, especially when I told them I'd travelled by Tube from Ealing. Only the cameraman ate it. The other two just did a clever manoeuvre with their spoons and tasted the soup.

The producer asked me where I'd bought the fish from, and his mood lifted when I told him Atari-Ya. It turned out he lived round the corner.

"They take their fish seriously there," he laughed. "One summer I went there to buy some tuna steaks for a barbecue, and the owner asked me what they were for, and then refused to sell them to me...he said they were far too good to waste on a barbecue!"

He threw a few questions at me, and told me about his own passion for food.

"I'd love to throw it all in and become a chef," he sighed, "get a job peeling spuds at Le Gavroche on £11,000 a year. But I've got a big mortgage, and two kids, and there's no way I could do it. I'm stuck in the rat race..."

He seemed so sincere, I half believed him. Then he asked what I did for a living, and I told him about the journalism. He liked that even less than the raw fish – he probably thought I was there to do an inside job.

"So why do you think you should be on the show?" he said finally.

"Because I'd make good TV?"

"That's what worries me," he said. "You know too much about the industry."

CHAPTER THREE

I carried on doing reporting shifts in Fleet Street as I waited for a cooking job to turn up. And I'd probably have stayed there, doorstepping for the devil and knocking golf balls into a mug every night until they carted me off with a gold watch and emphysema, if it hadn't been for the paper's night news editor Julian Bashford.

Sir Julian, as we liked to call him, was an eccentric old bird, and far too good for this world. He was the only person in the office who didn't think I was mad for trying to make it as a professional chef. He kept saying he was looking forward to an invite when I got my three stars.

But then he'd lived more than most of them, and was far less bitter and cynical. When he was my age, he'd walked to India, got as far as Istanbul, and ended up working as sports editor on an English language paper for three years. He didn't even like sport. After his flat-mate disappeared in the middle of the night, he fled the country and carried on walking to India.

He was a dark horse and full of the most amazing stories. Occasionally, a Spanish woman would call and cry down the phone when he told us to say he wasn't there.

"Unrequited love, I'm afraid," he would explain afterwards.

Although he had no interest in cooking, he was incredibly knowledgeable about food. He introduced me to Alan Davidson, author of the Oxford Companion To Food. At the time, I thought I knew everything that was worth knowing about food, and I hadn't even heard of Davidson.

The discovery was a revelation. Sir Julian knew him through his university days at Oxford. He told me how Davidson's food writing career was sparked when he was working as a diplomat in Tunis. His wife would come home from the market and say she didn't know what any of the fish were.

Davidson couldn't find a cookbook listing the local varieties, so he wrote one for her. The work – originally called Seafish Of Tunisia And The Central Mediterranean – eventually found its way to Elizabeth David. She passed it on to Penguin Books, who published it in 1972 under the much snappier title Mediterranean Seafood.

Sir Julian had every copy of Davidson's Petits Propos Culinaires journal of food studies and history – even the ones now out of print. I only wish I'd met the man. His writing was so lovingly detailed and painstakingly researched – even in the early days. It was in stark contrast to my early efforts.

My first newspaper job was writing a recipe column for a weekly paper. I used to make up the 100-word introductory flannel, talking about stews that dated back to Chaucer, the aphrodisiacal qualities of nettle soup, and dishes named after made-up minstrels.

For Newbury Pork Chops, I'd written: "This traditional country recipe dates back to a time when only the fattest and most succulent pork would be used. Newbury pigs were taken through the woods to sniff out truffles, and some chefs would add one or two to enrich the flavour..."

I had no idea whether there were even any truffles in Newbury. About the only thing I knew about the place was it had a racecourse. But it all went horribly wrong when I went travelling to South America. I'd written up the recipes beforehand, and each week my mother sent one in.

But I got held up in Colombia and ran out of recipes. My mother covered for me for a while, dutifully copying out recipes from cookbooks, until she did one for chocolate cake and the editor got calls from readers saying their cakes had come out "as flat as kipper's piss". It turned out she had forgotten to put the eggs in.

Two decades later, I was still doing the odd bit of food writing. But I wanted to cook for a living – not write about it. Most of my days were spent at the paper, and I'd stare at the grey-haired hacks around me doing the same job day after day, with no prospect of promotion, and I knew I had to get out. If I didn't do it now, I told myself, I never would.

One night, I had a drunken chat with Colin, who'd got me the job in the first place. We were sitting in a car outside a mansion in Eastbourne. We had no idea why we were there. They just told us to give the newsdesk a ring if a red Ferrari arrived. I hated jobs like that. It could be anyone from a celebrity to the head of a cocaine cartel. They never let you know too much – that way you couldn't tip off other papers.

Colin knew I was almost as unhappy as he was, and spent the night trying to convince me to leave journalism and become a chef.

"You've got the talent – I've seen it," he said. "That chicken curry you made the other night was great!"

"Really?" I said, my mood lifting slightly.

A red car appeared. It wasn't a Ferrari.

"I don't know why you don't go for it. Why don't you go down to Cornwall and work in a kitchen? You love it down there..."

I continued nodding and sipping from my hip-flask. In my semi-inebriated state it all seemed so easy. Just pack my bags and drive off to the coast, the oyster-breeze in my nostrils.

"I just wish I had a gift or a passion for something. You don't know what it's like if you haven't..." he said.

He was right. Cooking was the only time I was happy. As I chopped onions on my grease-spattered work surface, all anxiety seemed to pass, and it was just me and the knife.

Cooking lulled me away from the stress of work, and the guilt of ruining people's lives. I'd really come to loathe foot-in-the-door journalism - nodding with sympathy at the grieving relatives, while scanning the mantelpiece for family photos, and wondering how many they'd hand over, and whether there'd be any left when the rest of the Fleet Street flying circus turned up. People do strange things when they are in shock. It's amazing how much some talk in the first few hours – that is why news editors like you to get their early. Other times I'd try to persuade them that the pain they were suffering could best be assuaged by opening their hearts to our readers.

Sometimes when I cooked, I'd be far away, running back from that beach in France, holding up the scallop like a small God. My heart bursting with joy at the thought of how delighted everyone would be with what I'd found.

I knew I'd never rest until I became a chef, or at least tried. I didn't want to end up in my 60s with painful regrets, like an old man sitting alone at a gay bar. I just wanted to run a seaside pub with a dining room and a roaring fire. Proper suet puddings, potted hare, treacle tart, and home-made chutneys. At times, it all seemed so possible.

WEEKS WENT by and then I walked into the office one night, and it all began to change. Rudgie, one of the senior subs, was coming towards me. It was too late to turn back. He was doing the odd stand-up gig, and was forever trying out his jokes on us.

"Hey Lennie," he said, "I've got one for you!"

I tried to look pleased. You always had to laugh at his tiresome gags. That way he found less faults in your copy.

"There's this female police officer, and she arrests this bloke for drink-driving. She goes through the spiel and says to him: 'Sir, you have the right to remain silent. Anything you say CAN and WILL be held against you.'"

Rudgie paused for far too long. He had no sense of timing.

"So what happened?" I said.

"He says: 'Tits!'"

I chuckled weakly until it became slightly uncomfortable, but that just spurred him on. He followed me down the corridor.

"What do donkeys get for lunch on Blackpool beach?"

"I've no idea."

"About half-an-hour..."

The reporters and subs were all talking about that evening's game between Norwich and Manchester City. Even some of the associate editors had come out of their holes to join in. Apparently, Delia Smith had tottered on to the pitch at half-time and shouted at the Norwich fans to pull their socks up, and become the twelfth man. They were watching replays of the toe-curling scene. Again. And again. And again.

"LET'S BE 'AVING YOU!!!" she'd squawked like some crazy aunt.

It was hideous to watch. Jeering Man City fans had then chanted: "There's only one Jamie Oliver." The early editions of the next day's papers were full of it. Our headline was: "Ooopsh...I sheem to have made a mishtake!" I'd never seen the editor, a die-hard Ipswich fan, so animated.

"Where are you?" he kept saying. "Let's be 'avin you!"

"Too much sherry trifle!" someone added.

A story came in on the wires from Iraq. One of the jobs of the night reporter was sending out SMS text message breaking news alerts. I pasted the agency copy in, subbed it down to less than 140 characters, and then got a couple of others to read it. You always made sure there was a second pair of eyes on it – that way you could share the blame if it was wrong.

There had been a few mistakes recently, and the editor had sent out an email saying he'd be "mightily pissed off" if it happened again. No-one knew what that meant, but no-one was taking any chances. He'd already sent out an email that week to 20 members of staff asking them if they were thinking of resigning for missing a story about Peter Andre.

But there had only been one sacking over an SMS mistake. An agency broke the Queen Mother's death, and when the correction came in, one of the reporters sent out another alert saying: "Queen Mother not dead" which raised a few titters in media columns. The previous month, he'd sent one out about a police shooting and wrote: "Police execute gunman" – which had upset Scotland Yard immensely.

I read through the news alert again, ticked the confirmation box, and then let the text fly out there: "SIX AMERICANS AMONG 500 PEOPLE DEAD IN TWO SUICIDE BLASTS IN NORTHERN IRAQI CITY OF TIKRIT, SADDAM'S HOMETOWN, US MILITARY SAYS."

I didn't have room for "American troops" but I thought people would get the gist. The others began to file out to the pub. The editor was trying to round them up.

"Let's be 'avin you!" he said. "Christ, it's like trying to herd cats!"

41

And then they all joined in again with the "where are yous?" I started banging the phones for Sir Julian. I stared at him from over my computer screen, imagining myself with his bald head, bad back and poor eyes. I was little more than 20 years away. My hairline less than 10.

"Umm, would you like a nice, umm, cup of tea?" he said.

He didn't have a fridge at home and used his drawer in the newsroom as a larder. Sometimes he'd hand out chocolate biscuits covered in fluff. They were always stuck together, and about five-years-old. Sometimes he gave you shortbread, and would pick out the mould, muttering: "Perfectly alright, perfectly alright." He had jars of pickled gherkins and walnuts, and tins of pilchards in there as well. I wondered what a molecular gastronomist would make with those. Ice cream probably.

He began foraging for napkins, sugar sachets, and plastic stirrers. Sir Julian was very particular about tea-making, and would serve each polystyrene cup with an empty one balanced on top to keep the heat in.

If you ever made one for him, he would dart up and yell: "No, on the boil!" and make you switch on the kettle again, and pour at the precise moment the switch clicked. He could talk for hours about how they served tea in different parts of the world.

"Have you ever had Indian tea?" he would ask. "They serve it with hot milk, and enough sugar for your spoon to stand up in!"

As well as being an old soak and a hack, he was also an expert on mushrooms and gave talks at universities. Apparently, there was a fungi named after him somewhere in the world. He talked a lot about truffles. I used to sit there glued to his words, my mind far away from the big news stories of the day

42

like Jordan eating grub worms in the jungle or the latest bust-up on Big Brother. He told me how the Egyptians coated truffles in goose fat and cooked them en papillote, and how people in the Middles Ages used to think they were the devil's work, and appeared where lightning struck.

But my favourite story was the one about a mycology convention in Buckinghamshire, and how he'd got into a row with an Italian fungi expert. Sipping his tea, steam fogging up his glasses, he'd recount the tale. I had serious doubts about whether it was true. He was a hack after all, but I enjoyed it anyway...

"He was a frightful Eye-tie, you know. We'd got into an argument at a pub in the, um, Chiltern Hills. Do you know it? Rupert Brooke used to go there. 'And is there honey still for tea?' I don't know – but a spot of scrambled eggs would do...

"There's a snug where you can, er, read his scribblings. I don't know if it's still there. Overlooks this chalk Celtic cross – they think someone carved it as a prank, built a couple of barrows next to it as well to fool everyone!

"Anyway, this truffle expert had had a few too many glasses of beer, and it ended with a frightful row about Rossini. He was an, um, acclaimed gastronome, you know – used to call the truffle the Mozart of mushrooms...

"The Italian said the composer had wept three times in his life. Um, once when his first opera failed. Once, the first time he heard Paganini play the violin, and once when a truffled goose fell overboard at a boating picnic.

"It seemed a minor detail at the time. I just, um, mentioned that in fact it was a truffled turkey that had fallen overboard, and for some reason he turned a dreadful shade of puce, and said there wasn't a damned thing he didn't know about Rossini.

"In fact, he said no man on Earth knew more about, um, Rossini than he did, and that questioning an Italian's knowledge of Rossini was an insult of the highest order...He'd gathered quite a, um, crowd by that stage, and began thrashing his cheque book around, demanding a wager...And then he collapsed and died in hospital. A heart attack! And do you know the worst of it Lennie?"

"No," I'd always say.

"It WAS a truffled goose."

Maybe truffles were the devil's work? Maybe Sir Julian was too? He never aged in all the time I was at the paper. I used to think he had a painting in the attic.

Sir Julian poured in the water - on the boil - and handed me my tea. And then a pickled gherkin.

"Um, milk here," he said, pulling out a carton from his drawer, and hovering his nose over it. "I think it might be, um, on the turn."

He fished out another gherkin, then stopped suddenly, and pulled a crumpled bus ticket from his pocket.

"Oh, I forgot to give you this! It's a...um...advertisement I saw in a window inviting applications for the position of commis chef..."

There was a number scrawled on one side and the name of a restaurant. Only the number was legible. Later that night, I walked over to one of the phones in the corner and dialled. An angry, stressed voice answered immediately.

"Hello, Bert's Bistro!"

"Hi there, I'm calling about the job you had in the window..."

"Which one?" he snapped.

44

A FEW days later I went along to meet Bert, the owner of a small French restaurant in central London. He had the face of a bloodhound, and a large belly hanging over his jeans. He resembled a grotesque Jeremy Clarkson effigy in a grubby blazer. After a quick handshake and a flash of his yellow teeth, he told me to go downstairs to meet the head chef in the kitchen.

"He's a bit mad," he warned me before wandering off to check the wine cellar with a glass in his hand.

The stairs bent round twice and ended in a door with a glass porthole. The main kitchen was about 10ft wide and 20ft long, and empty as far as I could see. A serving hatch led through to a stove area. I could hear lids rattling, pans crashing and the occasional venomous curse.

I poked my head round. A scary-looking bulldog of a man was in there, surrounded by bubbling pots and pans. He was dressed in stained chef whites and had a dish-cloth slung over one shoulder. My respectful coughs were drowned out by the roar of the extractor fan. He picked up a chopper, hacked through a rabbit carcass, and then spotted me lurking in the doorway.

He stared at me with a calm dangerous look, holding my gaze for about an hour more than was necessary. Then he introduced himself, tapped my beer gut, and leered: "Don't worry; we'll soon get rid of that!"

For the next ten minutes, Grant whirled round the kitchen, boasting about how many jobs he was doing. He looked light on his feet like a boxer. I wondered whether that was how he'd got his broken nose.

"You see, that's what cooking's about – it's about TIME MANAGEMENT, overseeing a number of jobs at the same time," he kept boasting.

I nodded and he began pointing at different pots.

"In there I've got risotto as it goes, there - the veal bones for the stock. I've got mirepoix in there browning for the fish stock. Bass bones in there. That's puy lentils for the guinea fowl dish. That big one's for the salmon ballotines...That's what it's all about – time fucking management. Doing a number of jobs at the same time. That's what makes a good chef!"

There was no-one else in the kitchen. Clearly the rest of the staff turned up later. He continued ranting, stirring and kicking oven doors shut with his steel-clad feet. He filled a huge stockpot with dried milk and water to poach the salmon ballotine, and suddenly grabbed a handful of milk powder and hurled it into a gas ring next to me. It burst into a mass of orange and purple flames. I jumped back and was almost half-way up the stairs by the time I'd regathered my senses.

"Shit yourself did yer?" he chuckled.

Then he rounded on me violently, and shoved me towards the stock pot. I thought he was going to dunk my head in.

"Do you know why I cook the salmon in dried milk and not real milk?"

I shook my head and shrugged my shoulders at the same time – a feat I've never been able to do since. I was already terrified of him.

"Because it's FUCKING CHEAPER!"

He picked up a knife sharpener, and began running a large blade through it in mid-air. It was one of those cheap sharpeners housewives use. The ones that leave crooked ruts in the blade. I could see the metal shavings in the air.

"That's what it's all about. Time management! Multi-tasking! You know what chef means?"

I did, but I sensed it was best not to give the right answer.

"It means CHIEF!" he snapped. "Are YOU a chef?"

"No, but..."

"That's right! You're NOT a chef."

And then he stopped suddenly and looked down at the knife. I looked away quickly. I'd never been good with the sight of blood. There was a savage wound to his left thumb, and then I saw what he'd done to his index finger. You could see the tooth-floss tendons through the red. He began mumbling instructions, gripping the work surface to stay upright.

"Take the risotto off in exactly a minute right, it's got to have a crunch to it, and lay it out on a tray and put it in the fridge...take the bones out of the oven and put them in the stockpot...take those lentils off in five minutes...remember, time man..."

He began to pass out, and I raced upstairs looking for the owner, and then found him in the wine cellar. Grant was laid out in the back of Bert's battered Mercedes and driven to hospital. I was left alone in the kitchen, trying to follow his instructions. The risotto needed to go in the oven...the bones in a tray. I could scarcely remember the rest.

Ten minutes later, a chef called Frank walked in. He had wiry hair and an easy-going manner, and didn't seem in the slightest bit surprised to see me there on my own. I explained what had happened, and he began rescuing dishes.

But it turned out he knew little more than me – he left the main section of the kitchen to Grant. He was far too scared to go in there. The only time he did was to make soda pancakes

47

for his apple dessert dish, and he always did that when Grant was out of the kitchen.

After a few minutes of stirring, he spotted the tray the veal bones had been roasted in. There were lumps of meat juice caramel stuck to the bottom.

"What did you do with the bones?"

"Put them in the pot..."

"You didn't deglaze it first! Oh Christ, he's not going to like that..."

Grant turned up about an hour later with a huge bandage on his left hand and a pack of pain killers in his right. He bragged how there had almost been a fight in A&E when Bert pushed him to the front of the queue, saying it was an emergency because he was doing service that night.

"It's like a fucking glove-puppet," Grant yelled, holding up his hand and making mouthing motions. "These are the bollocks, though," he added, opening a pack of pink horse pills.

His pupils were dark and glazed like a drugged tiger. Then his eyes fixed on the hatch and Frank's bobbing head.

"Oy! Frank you muppet, what are you doing in there?"

He lurched off through the doorway. There were lowered voices and something about stock, and then an explosion, and Grant appeared, with Frank padding along at his heels like a whipped dog. The head chef's face looked drug-addled and ugly.

"I could have SWORN I told you what to do," he hissed.

"You were passing out!" I squealed like a high-pitched Stan Laurel.

48

It went quiet for a moment as I waited for the brandings and punches. I'd be lucky to escape with a mild kneecapping or waterboarding – this man had already bragged about how he'd been trained in "the SAS of kitchens".

I was saved by Frank.

"You passed out?" he said before he could stop himself.

Grant glared at us like a lunatic on a crowded Tube. We scuttled backwards, but he managed to grab Frank with his good hand.

"I don't fucking believe it! I come back in here with this on to help you out and that's all the thanks I get. If that had been you Frank, you'd be like piss on the floor! You'd have had a week off, shacked up with your German girlfriend!"

Frank looked down at the tiles like a scolded schoolboy.

Somehow we managed to get through service, with Grant chopping and stirring one-handed. By the end, his bandage was covered in a patina of spilled sauces and oils. It looked like an artist's palette rag.

I WOKE the next morning, and fell back into the sheets, awaiting the day's first assault. And then I remembered the cheffing job. Something inside me lifted, and I wasn't even dreading working at the paper that evening. The first shovels of earth from the escape tunnel had been dug. It might have been terrifying, but these were my first tentative steps as a paid chef. Or at least I hoped it was paid – we hadn't discussed money yet.

I cooked at the restaurant the following evening and the madness and bullying started all over again. But there was no denying Grant could cook, and that I could learn a lot from him - if I could last the pace and wasn't chopped up and put in the freezer for pie fillings. Even one-handed, he managed to plough through boxes of fish and meat quicker than I could peel a bucket of potatoes – while keeping up a mantra about how "fucking slow" I was.

I'd read and heard about chefs like Grant – the racists, the bullies, and the dry-humping degenerates. He was a product of London's notoriously tough Michelin-starred kitchens – before they were partly cleaned up by HR (human remains) departments. Those hell holes were run on fear - nobody saw anything and nobody did anything to stop it. The only reprieve from the institutionalised bullying was that one day it would be your turn to dish it out. And Grant had waited a long time for his.

He was almost as obsessive about football as he was about cooking, and kept repeating stories from his Chelsea days. He told us about the fear and pride he felt as an 18-year-old when they were cut off from the pack, and rushed by a gang of 50 Spurs fans. They stood firm, outnumbered, yelling at them to run faster. Sensing he was about to leg it, one of his hooligan comrades grabbed him and yelled in his face: "You're Chelsea now!"

Grant took a pounding, and was in hospital for weeks. But he'd been accepted into the tribe. He told us about an away match against Watford when they spotted Sir Elton John, or Reggie as they began chanting, in the stands. With military precision, hundreds of Chelsea fans produced cucumbers and pelted the executive box.

"It was lime-green by the end," he gloated.

Grant was also obsessed with Great Britain and her former glories, and passionately proud that both his grandfathers had "fought the Hun". He saw immigrants as work-shy criminals, and had a particular hatred for East Europeans, mainly because so many ended up in his kitchen.

But the people he detested most were the Germans. His hero was Sir Arthur "Bomber" Harris. Whenever we were hit hard during service, he would draw feeble comparisons with the Second World War.

"Those boys, when they were fighting the Germans, they didn't give up, did they!" he'd shout at us. "They didn't turn over and get shagged up the arse! They stood strong, and took it like a man.

"And now I've got that twat," he'd shout at Frank or me, "whingeing because he can't get a couple of plates out!"

Grant would continually tease Frank about his German girlfriend, saying he was "a traitor for shagging the Hun". Sometimes he'd tear a menu off the wall and chase him round the kitchen with it.

"You're fucking me up the arse the way you cook," he'd yell. "That's my name there where it says head chef! I might as well cross it out and write 'C***' in big letters next to it. Here, go and give this to the customers!"

He kept repeating the same stories and nearly all of them were racist, homophobic, or downright perverted. I kept my head down, and tried to shut out the continual shouting and threats. It was a different stress to the snake pit of tabloid journalism. There was bullying there too, but professional cooking was all about trying to keep up no matter what was thrown at you. But it certainly gave me an adrenaline kick. The closest I'd got to it as a hack was having dogs set on me on death knocks. But that soon stopped when I learned to carry bacon in my pocket. Even the most ferocious dogs like bacon.

I started working at the bistro two or three evenings a week, and some weekends. I spent the first few weeks doing simple jobs for Frank on the starters and desserts section. With

Grant watching my every move through the hatch, I quickly had the kitchen basics drummed into me.

Few things irritated him more than me using the wrong type of chopping board for the wrong job. It was green for vegetables and fruit, red for meat, blue for fish, and white for dairy. But I kept getting it wrong to start with in my quest to pick up speed, and even Frank was understandably annoyed when I diced raw tuna on his dessert board one day.

I was also shown how to set up my board, laying a damp cloth or piece of towelling under it to stop it sliding around as I chopped. Hygiene was another essential. Once when I put a tray of raw chicken at the top of the fridge, Grant went berserk saying it had dripped down on to the cream. But I couldn't see anything.

I was told to clean and go as I worked – wiping down the whole work surface and putting everything back in the fridge, and cling-filming and labelling it with that day's date, before moving on to the next job.

Other things he picked me up on came as a surprise. I thought I knew how to chop onions. But the first thing Grant looked at was my amateur knife skills. It was all stuff I should have learned at catering college. He showed me how to cut off the top of each onion and slice it in half through the root - making it easier to peel. You make regular cuts in the onion, stopping each slice just short of the root, while holding the vegetable with your left hand (if you're right-handed) like a claw, so that your fingers are safely tucked away, and the blade just brushes the flat of your knuckles.

You turn the onion 90 degrees, and with the knife horizontal, make a few cuts sideways towards the root. Then you slice downwards from right to left, and watch the pieces fall away into tiny dice. It was great the first time it happened. When finely chopping herbs like parsley, I learned to hold the point of the blade with my left hand and the handle in my right, and work away in a rocking motion.

He also showed me different vegetable cuts, but this took far longer to learn. For brunoise (small dice) you cut the veg into 2mm-wide slices using a mandolin, and then trim each piece into a rectangle, before cutting it into 2mm-wide strips lengthways. You turn the strips round, holding a few at a time, and cut them into 2mm x 2mm square dice. Mine were very clumsy to start with, but Grant's looked like they'd been done by machine, which in a way they had.

For thin sticks of julienne, the veg is cut into slices the same as brunoise, but then trimmed and cut into 2mm-wide strips about 3cm long. Grant loved using basil as a garnish, and would get me to roll up the leaves and cut them into perfect julienne shreds. It was harder than it sounded, getting them as precise as he wanted. And often he'd hurl my efforts in the bin and get me to start again.

"No, they should look like green pubes! You're lucky – when I was learning, they got me to cut carrier bags full of the stuff."

When I mentioned that later to Frank, he said: "That's bollocks. No restaurant needs that much basil!"

I was also shown how to roughly chop onion, celery, carrot, and leek for the mirepoix base for the stocks and soups. I was much better at that.

During service, I was put on garnish and would run around frying chips, and heating rice and vegetables in the microwave. Sometimes I'd help out with the desserts. My prep duties included making the crispy confit duck salad and the sage beignets.

For the former, you marinade duck legs in sea salt, black pepper, honey and sesame seeds for a day, and keep some of the mix aside for the salad. The next day, you drain off the moisture drawn out by the salt - what Grant affectionately termed "duck's piss" - then wash the legs and dry them carefully. You then cook them in duck fat in a low oven for three hours until the meat falls away from the bone. For service, you blast them in a hot oven for 20 minutes until crispy.

The duck was delicious, and I'd always try to steal some from plates when he wasn't looking – until he caught me with my mouth full, that is.

I made the salad by cutting Victoria plums into julienne strips and mixing them with chopped spring onion and a tablespoon of the marinade. You cut wafer-thin slices of cucumber on the mandolin, arrange them in a circle on the plate and heap the plum salad in the centre. You cut the duck leg in two, through the ball joint, and balance the thigh on top and the drumstick next to it.

The sage beignets for the sea bass dish were wonderful, and people sometimes ordered them as a side dish. You make the tapenade filling by mixing equal proportions of finely chopped anchovy fillets, black olives, capers, and a little fresh rosemary. You then match up similar-sized pairs of sage leaves, and smear a teaspoon of the tapenade over one leaf and sandwich them together.

I stored them on greaseproof paper in the freezer until needed. For service, I'd make batter using plain flour, salt, and expensive wheat beer. I'd dip the beignets in flour and then the batter and deep-fry them for a couple of minutes until golden.

Using the deep-fryer meant entering Grant's domain, and he also kept me busy ferrying his dishes to the dumb waiter. It was old and rickety, and some of the stacked dishes had toppled over by the time they got up to the dining room. The base was covered in night light candles to keep the plates warm, but they did nothing for the salads. It was my job to light the candles before service, and I'd light them ten at a time with a blowtorch.

After a few more days, I took a couple of days off, and returned to the paper to earn some money. I still didn't know how much I'd be getting paid, and whenever I tried to bring it up, Bert changed the subject.

CHAPTER FOUR

Sir Julian was interested to know how I was getting on at the bistro, and I'd give him regular updates. One day I went in and found him chuckling over an email he'd been sent by a stringer in Moscow. It was apparently a true account of a radio conversation between Americans and Spanish off the Galician coast, as recorded by a Russian radio ham.

Spanish: This is C-853, please turn 15 degrees south, in order to prevent collision with us...

US: We advise you to turn 15 degrees north. You are moving directly towards us at 25 sea miles per hour.

Spanish: Negative. We advise you to move 15 degrees south to prevent collision.

US: This is Captain Mark Edwards, Commander of USS Lincoln. We have two cruisers, six fighters, four submarines and numerous support ships. I advise you to change your bearing 15 degrees north, or I shall be forced to take the necessary measures to protect our ship...

Spanish: You are speaking to Juan Manuel Escobar. There are two of us, two bottles of beer and a sleeping canary. We are not going to turn off anywhere, because we are lighthouse C-853 on the coast of Galicia. Will you please head 15 degrees south...

I WORKED at the kitchen at the weekend, and Grant took a rare day off, so I did Sunday lunch with Frank. We were only trusted with bought-in stuffing and Aunt Bessie's Yorkshire puddings, but we made a reasonably good fist of it, and Bert even bought us a drink. It was great cooking without the continual screaming and bullying, and I imagined how enjoyable it would be running my own restaurant without a head chef breathing down my neck.

But when I got in the next day, Grant was in a terrible temper. He told me Frank had left the fryer on all night, and Bert's ex-wife had been sleeping upstairs. He told me the story about five times, getting more and more worked up every time he told it.

"He could have fucking killed her! I would have throttled his neck! I laid into him on the phone, and he kept saying 'sorry'. So I said: 'What are you going to do, say sorry to Bert after you've killed his ex-wife?'"

But Bert didn't seem too bothered. He kept telling Grant to calm down, saying he didn't want to lose Frank because it was difficult holding on to chefs. I wasn't in the least bit surprised. I don't know how Frank managed to stick the job. It was bad enough for me, and I was only working there three days a week or so, and mostly then I'd only do one service.

Frank hated cooking – to him it was just a job. He looked at me oddly when I talked about wanting to become a chef. "Why do you want to leave your cushy job at a newspaper? I'd kill for a job like that!"

His passion was music. He'd been in a band with his brother and sister, but was kicked out. But he wasn't bitter about it. He freely admitted he hadn't got the talent. He talked about the band proudly, and said they were on the verge of success. I wasn't sure if it was just talk or wishful thinking. But a year or so later, the band had taken the country by storm, and I hoped Frank had become part of it somehow.

We would occasionally drink with his brother Neil, the drummer in the band, in the Irish pub across the road after work. He'd always be sat on his own at the bar, gulping down pints of Stella. He was a lonely, sad character, and looked like a tramp with his long hair and beard. It was strange to see him on TV. I wondered whether the success would change him, or if he'd just move on to pints of champagne.

The only other person in the kitchen was the pot wash Jerzy. But he didn't always come in and Frank and I would have to keep on top of the washing up while getting the plates out. Jerzy was a huge Polish man, who always did the minimum he could get away with. Despite being a plongeur, and therefore at the bottom of the traditional kitchen pecking order, he saw me as below him because he could do all the cooking tasks better than me, and was called in when I lagged behind.

Occasionally, he would phone up an hour before service and demand a pay rise or threaten not to come in. This would infuriate Grant and he would yell insults down the phone until Jerzy turned up sometime later.

One day, Jerzy let slip that his family had servants. Grant seized on it straight away. He always spoke to Jerzy in broken English.

"Oh, so you rich boy!" he sniped. "You had servants! So everything you do here now for me, they did for you!"

Then his eyes narrowed as he spewed the next bit of venom.

"Well, you're in Blightie now Jerzy – you're nothing here! You wash up when I tell you to..."

"No! No! I'm not rich. No servants," Jerzy kept saying, but he knew the damage had been done.

Grant walked over to our side of the kitchen in triumph

"You got to watch those Eastern Europeans," he told us. "What are Labour doing handing out passports to that lot for? They're gonna take the place over, you wait and see. Give it a few years and there won't be jobs for the rest of us!"

Frank and I just nodded whenever he ranted, which was pretty much all the time. There was nothing else you could do. Like many head chefs, he didn't understand the concept of conversation – our job was just to listen, agree, and pretend to laugh.

FRANK'S PUNISHMENT for the fryer incident was not being allowed to leave early to go to Neil's gig. The band were playing in front of several record companies, and had been told if they drew a big enough crowd over three nights they'd get signed. It was easily their biggest gig yet, and Frank desperately wanted to be there for support.

He had tears in his eyes when he told me about it. Grant was delighted, and kept telling him to stop sulking. Service was busy, and then Bert came down to tell us two tables of eight had come in at once. Grant started shouting, saying he wanted all the starters out in five minutes. I was finding it increasingly difficult to bite my tongue, and pointed out that they hadn't even ordered yet.

"Oooh, they haven't ordered yet!" he replied. "We can't start until we know what they're having. Oooh, I think I'm going to cry! Well get a few fucking ducks on! What do you think our boys did on the beaches? Sit around eating ice creams? And now the Krauts are trying to do it again – take over Europe and get rid of the pound. We're all going to be talking German soon. And that twat's already got himself a German fucking girlfriend!"

"I've told you about that," said Frank.

It was the first time I'd heard him answer back.

Grant was delighted with the reaction. He put his arms around his sous chef, and started thrusting his hips.

"This tart you're boning, right, is it like being in a porno? Does she yell out 'Ja! Ja! Ja!' like a posh bird?"

"Piss off," Frank said, pulling away.

I got mine a couple of weeks later. When I'd started, Grant had warned me about not using mobile phones in the kitchen. I forgot all about mine and it went off during service. He ran round to our side and gave me the hairdryer treatment.

"What did I say? I don't want mobiles going off during service!"

Then he grabbed my phone and threw it in the deep-fat fryer.

"Go on, answer it now!" he bawled.

But despite the stress and torment, and the many times I thought about ditching it all in, I learned a lot at the bistro. I was proud of my new knife skills, and would practise cutting carrots into brunoise on my days off. But it was the sauces I was most proud of.

Grant boasted about how people travelled half-way across London just to try his gravy. And pretty soon I was making the beef, chicken, fish and vegetable stocks, and demi-glace reductions without much complaint. He told me how making stock was the most important job in the kitchen, and once you had good quality stocks you could make all manner of sauces, meat glazes, and jellies, and that popping in a few tablespoons of demi-glace to the cooking juices when pan-frying a steak or chop completely transforms the dish.

For veal stock, I'd place marrow bones and braising steak in a tray and roast them for about an hour until well-browned. I'd slice three large onions in half and blacken the cut-side over a gas flame - releasing a lovely caramel flavour. I'd fry the mirepoix and tomato puree in a stockpot, and then deglaze the oven tray and add the rich gravy, water and bones.

I'd bring the stock to the boil, simmer it slowly, and skim it from time to time to clear the liquid. I'd then add a garlic head, cut in half horizontally so that all the cloves were exposed, bay leaves, black peppercorns, thyme, juniper

60

berries, and a bottle of red wine and continue to simmer and skim.

Other stocks were made in the same way by substituting pork bones, chicken carcasses, lamb bones, and pheasant and venison bones for game stock. For white chicken stock, I'd use uncooked chicken, and for brown, I'd roast the bones first, throwing in onion skins for extra colour. Grant never used fish heads for fish stock, claiming it made it cloudy. But other chefs I've spoken to since say that is nonsense.

After hours of simmering and skimming, I'd strain the liquid through a fine-meshed sieve, and either store it in the fridge as stock or reduce it by two-thirds or more to make a meat glaze that was so syrupy it coated the back of a spoon and set in the fridge like quince paste.

AFTER SIX weeks working part-time at the restaurant, Grant took me out to the yard for some sort of assessment. We sat near the bins on one of the patio tables they used in the summer. He said I could do everything in the kitchen, but I was just "too fucking slow". It came as no surprise; he'd been saying the same thing every few minutes for the past six weeks.

The secret of professional cooking, he said, was all about speed (and God knows he'd taken enough of the stuff). It was a far cry from bumbling around a domestic kitchen, picking herbs from the garden, scanning recipe books for ideas, with breaks for coffee and the occasional blank stare at the crossword. It was all in the mise-en-place. If you hadn't got everything prepped before service, you were screwed. And to get everything prepped, you had to be fast.

At one point, Bert stuck his head round the door, wondering why we weren't working. He was about to say something, and then saw the scowl on Grant's face and thought better of it. The pair hadn't talked for two days. Messages were being relayed by Bert's business partner John, a Welsh accountant who spent most of his time propping up the bar.

The row started when one of the regular customers asked for her tuna tartare to be cooked, and Grant picked up a knife steel and waved it at Bert, and told him to get out of the kitchen. John was called in to mediate, but Grant had even less respect for him than he did for Bert. He called him "the kiddie fiddler" behind his back because he owned hundreds of toddler rides you see at the entrances to supermarkets.

"Listen Grant old boy, I know you won't like this, but Bert wants to take the tuna tartare dish off the menu..."

"WHY?" Grant snapped.

"Because there's talk...now I'm not saying this mind, you of all people know how partial I am to the tartare, but Bert says it doesn't go down too well with the more squeamish customers like."

"Then why do they fucking order it if they don't know what it is!"

"Well, you know what bloody customers are like..."

"And anyway, what does Bert know about food? Here's a clue – two words. The first word is 'fuck' and the second word is 'all'."

Bert was looking fidgety as we sat outside. There was an uncomfortable silence for a few seconds. He glanced round at the rubbish piled up in the yard and then back at us.

"Hey, stop taking leaves from that bay tree. It's only got about five leaves left – that was a wedding present, you know!"

He feigned a mortally-wounded expression, and then wiped his nose. I looked down at the small, withered tree with its brown, curled leaves. It was a perfect symbol of Bert's failed marriages. It was his aspidistra.

"Twat!" said Grant as Bert's head disappeared.

He lit another cigarette and stabbed at the plant with the tip. He appeared to be in no rush to go back in. I thought he was going to ask me for money, and began preparing excuses. I still hadn't been paid yet.

Then he told me about his money problems, and I knew it was coming. He said he had started going to Gamblers' Anonymous meetings to sort himself out. His branch was run by an old Irish boy, who stuck his head in the oven to escape his gambling debts, but was saved when the money ran out in the gas meter. And then spent the rest of his life asking people what the odds were of that.

"Cheapest club to join, the most expensive to leave! They say if you carry on, you'll end up in prison, the gutter, or the fucking river."

I gave him £50 and he said he'd pay me out of his next wage packet.

I STILL hadn't been paid after three months at the restaurant. Every time I brought it up with Bert, he blamed "that useless Welsh bastard John" or made excuses about admin problems, or the computer breaking down, or aliens invading, and then disappeared, wiping his nose as he went. I wanted to be a chef, but I was sick of working that hard for nothing, especially if I was lining Bert's septum.

One night after service, I confronted him with Frank in the bar. Bert was more wrecked and wired than usual, and showing off in front of his regulars.

"I'm not talking about money at 11.30 at night!" he yelled.

I thought about making a scene, but just shook my head. "I'd forget all about this place if I were you," said Frank as we walked out.

I parked the car, and then walked under the railway bridge to my flat. I could hear the occasional splat of pigeon shit around me. In all the times I'd walked under there, I'd never been hit once.

I trudged past the church hall, where they held Gamblers' Anonymous meetings, and thought about Grant and the money again, and how I'd miss cooking at the bistro – even if it was all madness. On the church board was a poster, saying: "What would YOU do if Jesus Christ arrived today?" Underneath someone had written: "Move St John to inside right and play him centre forward."

I went into the office the next day. There was an email about a story I'd written about a Premiership footballer laying into a student in a late-night bar. It was from the player's agent, and one of the bosses had sent it out on staff messages so everyone could have a giggle. The letter was marked "not for publication".

It said: "R did not act physically or verbally. The toe-rag student wound him up. R is a hard nut and if he'd wanted to put the c*** down he would have. That prick would not have been posing for pretty boy pictures in your paper within hours of a beating from R."

I knew from the tone there was nothing to worry about. Half the stories in the paper were made up anyway. But I was still sent out on a death knock to Soho.

There was no answer on the intercom, or at the neighbours' flats. I waited in the cold and damp for a few hours, then there was a cloudburst and torrential rain, so I ducked inside a Chinese restaurant. The place was packed, and I was looking round trying to spot a table near the window, so I could keep an eye on the flat's communal entrance, when a furious-looking waiter pounced on me.

"What you waaaannn?"

I noticed people had stopped eating and were looking at me.

"Table for one," I said slightly pompously.

The waiter eyed me suspiciously.

"We gorr no table for one! You go down stair!"

Then he was off in his shiny black shoes, scuttling waiters.

I stood there for a moment, confused. I didn't like crowded restaurants at the best of times. The sniggers from nearby tables faded, and I spotted a staircase leading down. At the bottom, I was met by another waiter.

"Hi there, how are you doing?" I said.

His hate-filled eyes bored into me. It felt like a scene from Merry Christmas Mr Lawrence.

"Wery busy!" he spat. "What you waaan?"

He was worse than the last one. People were listening intently, pretending not to notice.

"Table for one, please."

"You got no frenn? You go upstair, he give you table!"

"He just told me to come down here!"

I was going red in the face, and it drove him on mercilessly like a shark sniffing blood.

"You go back!" he shouted. "We got no table for one downstair!"

The tables around me exploded, and I walked back up the stairs humiliated, my back covered in laughter darts. I was furious, and penning a complaint letter in my head: "Dear Sir/Madam, I am writing in the strongest possible terms about the rudeness and downright insolence of two of your waiters..."

Then the manager shouted something at me. I hurried out, and looked up at the sign. It was Wong Kei – a place famed for the rudeness of its staff. Those mean bastards wouldn't have got sacked as I'd hoped - they'd have got a pay rise. They'd probably even frame my letter and hang it on the toilet wall.

TWO DAYS later, Grant was on the phone trying to persuade me to come back in. He said he had an envelope of money for me.

"I haven't opened it, so I don't know how much is in there," he added.

I went back that night. Bert attempted a grin as I walked in. I changed into my whites, and opened the envelope. There was £82.47 in cash in there. It probably worked out at less than 50p an hour, but I couldn't be bothered to complain. I just needed to find a new cheffing job, and it would be better to say I was already working somewhere else.

Grant was in an especially foul mood the following night because Chelsea were playing Barcelona in the Champions League, and he hadn't been given the night off despite working 21 days in a row. I couldn't help feeling sorry for him.

It wasn't just sympathy for him, of course. It was the realisation that my decision to retrain as a chef meant giving

66

up everything else in my life. I knew I'd have even less free time if I ran my own place. But then I suppose my social life would revolve around the business, wouldn't it? I could be like Floyd in his heyday in Bristol, sitting down at customers' tables and regaling them with stories as I helped myself to their wine, or glugged brandies and sneaked them on to their bills.

Grant got me to work on his side, plating up, so he could concentrate on the game on a jabbering radio in the corner. He told me he'd put a week's wages on a Chelsea win, at odds of 4/1. All he could talk about was how he was going to spend the money at the knocking shop over the road.

I had a very bad feeling. There was a good reason the bookies had made Barcelona odds-on favourites to win. Bert came into the kitchen looking worried too. He was obviously wondering how a Blues defeat would affect service. A blob of snot rolled down from his nose. I just hoped to God that Grant hadn't had some as well.

I went round to get some herbs, and Frank whispered: "I'm so glad it's not me working over there with him tonight. Sorry mate!" He patted me on the back like a condemned prisoner as I returned to the seething Chelsea sauna.

Grant was chanting at the top of his voice, and banging a blue chopping board on the work surface. I could see Frank whimpering through the hatch. We both knew that one day Grant would go on a knife-wielding killing spree. Prisons are full of chefs like him. And it was more likely to happen that night than any other. I could see the newspaper headlines already - Crazed Chelsea Chef Butchers Staff With Chopper. Bert looked in again and eyed his head chef nervously. They were still barely on speaking terms.

"Tonight's the night then," he said.

"Fucking too right! We're going to show you Arsenal boys how to do it!"

Two orders came in for bar food, and I started frying chips and grilling burgers as the whistle blew and Grant screamed: "COME ON!"

The game started at a furious pace, and I tried to match my speed to the commentary - chopping lettuce, slicing buns, wiping down work surfaces, and doing anything to dispel my feeling of impending doom. I didn't want to give Grant the slightest excuse.

It started well, but then my heart took a pounding, and felt like it was about to explode, when Barca fumbled an early open goal. Grant stopped in mid-flow, and the fish he had just flipped seemed to stop with him. "Yesssss!" he screamed a moment later, punching the air.

My hands were tingling, my stomach was heaving, and my legs were wobbling like a crab on stilts. The orders piled in and I took a nasty burn on the thumb, which quickly bubbled into a yellow gobstopper, when Grant passed me a red-hot metal duck plate.

"That's not my fault," he said quickly, "where's your fucking cloth chef?"

My thumb was throbbing as I pushed on, and then the atmosphere in the kitchen lifted. Chelsea were playing the ball about. It was goal-end stuff. Joe Cole was on to a good one, and my heart raced madly with hope, and then fell back from my throat as the ball bounced harmlessly away for a goal kick.

"Fuck!" shouted Grant, throwing a ladle across the room.

It was still goalless when the order for the big table came in. Grant roared at Frank to get the starters out. It was a pre-order so there were no excuses. I started chopping onions,

68

knowing that for the next ten minutes the attention would be away from me. I listened to the commentary as Grant disappeared next door and began screaming at Jerzy. I could barely hear the radio, but the pundits were squabbling about something...

"Anyway, Barcelona are on the attack...and have they won a corner? They have. It's very difficult actually to concentrate when there's so much activity in front of us - it's ludicrous. Oh, I'm not going to argue with him, have you seen the size of him?"

I threw the onions in a pan with some chopped mushrooms, and checked the fryer.

"You sit wherever you want, sir! Thirteen-and-a-half minutes to half-time, the corner's taken and it's a free header over the crossbar, which you couldn't have seen Ray."

I whizzed up the cream veloute to make a foam.

"Oh here we go again! The stewards have really got to get their act together here, Ray. Anyway, it's still Barcelona nil, Chelsea nil. Goodness that guy is enormous, a sort of Spanish sumo wrestler."

"He's certainly not the cox in the boat race is he Mike!"

Grant returned as the commentator's voice hit fever pitch. I looked around for the nearest knife.

"Now Chelsea have got three players in a forward position! It goes towards Duff, and Duff is onside. Here's Damien Duff...great cross in."

"Own goal! It's an own goal! Chelsea not only have an away goal, they have the lead at the Nou Camp!"

Grant threw his arms around me, and splattered my face with saliva.

"COME ON!"

Frank drew the sign of a cross on his chest and looked up at the ceiling. Grant smeared bone marrow and herbs on the eye fillets, threw them in the oven, kicked the door shut, and danced around the kitchen. Bert ducked in again, hearing the screams, and shot back out.

"Gooner!" Grant shouted after him. He turned up the volume on the radio. Frank was mouthing things from across the hatch, but I couldn't hear him.

"Fury here from the Barcelona supporters who sense that Chelsea are wasting time. And they took as long as they could to take that free kick...Duff on the right-hand side, Duff's cross, left-footed towards the back post..."

That was it – a Chelsea goal to seal the game. Surely we were saved?

But then the crowd started screaming like banshees. It rose like a howling, demonic wind and swept through the kitchen. Frank and I looked at each other. Something was definitely wrong...

"Belletti was there, it was casual...Drogba too...Drogba's gone down inside the six-yard box...Anders Frisk is standing there and he's given...it's a red card! That looks like a red card!"

Grant's chants trailed off in confusion. Thousands of fans were screaming, and soon he was screaming with them.

"Drogba, Didier Drogba!! Has been sent off for his lunge in at goalkeeper Victor Valdes...So Chelsea are leading here in the Nou Camp by a goal to nil with what...35 minutes in the game to play, with ten men!"

70

"BLIND C***!" Grant shouted at a referee he couldn't see.

I got back to work on the plates. The game went deathly quiet. There was a deadening crack as though someone had wound up an antique clock too far.

"I don't believe it! What were they doing? The Chelsea back four were just standing there!"

And then came the sound I'd been dreading all day - Spanish cheers.

"And all of a sudden, with the substitute coming on, he's changed the game completely! One-one, would you believe it! There was a dummy, and a ball played in to Maxi Lopez, and he put it exactly, the only place really, that Cech could cover, and he still didn't save it."

It was all over, and I knew it. The kill was quick, and seven minutes later, Eto'o rifled home to light up the Nou Camp. I stood there frozen over the chopping board. The commentary was almost drowned out by Grant.

"I FUCKING KNEW I shouldn't have worked tonight!" he screamed.

The final whistle was like the sound of an executioner's axe. An away goal was good for Chelsea. But Grant's money was gone. I looked round in slow motion like they do in horror films.

Grant had his head in his hands. And then he seemed to decide on something. It was probably the realisation that he'd worked the whole of the previous week, putting up with complaints about his tuna tartare, for nothing. He hurled a frying pan to the floor, and then began smashing plates against the wall. I ran into the starters section. Frank had picked up a rolling pin, thinking it was Grant racing round.

71

The head chef followed me in and hurled a bowl of flour into the air. Frank and I backed away slowly. The maniac began sweeping plates off the starter's section. Then he picked up a fork and ambled towards us. There was a blank look in his eyes and no escape route. We had to get past him to get out.

Suddenly, there was movement from behind, and Jerzy flew past and floored Grant with a punch. Jerzy stood over him, looking down. Grant was out cold, but Frank and I were taking no chances. We ran out into the yard and shinned over the fence before he could recover.

That was the last day I worked there. I drove past three weeks later and there was a 'for sale' sign up outside. The receivers had moved in and taken over the building.

CHAPTER FIVE

I went back to doing full-time shifts at the paper, and applied for a few cooking jobs. One day I had lunch with a fat man called Boris. He was the editor-at-large (a title that owed more to his size than salary) on a catering magazine I occasionally wrote a column for.

I told him all about the bistro, and wanting to retrain as a chef, and asked him for advice. He knew all the top chefs in London, and said he was sure he could get me some work experience somewhere. Then for some reason, whether it was the wine or just a misguided belief in my cooking abilities, he suggested I write a book about training to be a chef. He said we should approach a publishing company he knew, and sell them the idea of me buying an old banger and driving to Spain, working in restaurants and writing about my experiences along the way.

"Spain's the food capital of the world," he said breathlessly, dripping shallot vinegar over another oyster and tilting his head back and swallowing with a rather disturbing look on his face.

He wiped his mouth with the back of his hand and his piggy eyes scanned our fruit de mer for more morsels. There were just a few sorry-looking whelks and winkles nestled in the melting ice on his side of the table. His trotter reached over and grabbed the crab I was saving.

"Do you mind old bean?"

I shook my head and he snatched the greasy nutcrackers and got to work on a large brown claw. There were white spindles of crab and lobster meat in his beard.

"It'll be brilliant. There are thousands out there who want to be chefs, but are too afraid to do it."

"Or too sane," I muttered

But Boris wasn't listening. He was off somewhere in one of his happy, gluttonous dreams, fondly remembering times his 20-stone bulk danced nimbly around the stove. He stopped suddenly and his narrow eyes glittered.

"Arm-chair chefs! That's it! It's for the **ARM-CHAIR CHEFS!** It'll be like those travel guides for people who are far too scared to actually hack their own way through the jungle, but are more than happy to read about someone else doing it!

"There are masses of foodies out there, obsessed with what goes on in a kitchen – how the professionals really do it – the tricks of the trade! Just look at the viewing figures for Masterchef! They'd like nothing more than to snuggle up in front of the fire, with the cat on their lap and a big mug of tea steaming away next to them, reading about the honest gruel of kitchen labour..."

He ordered a brandy.

"You'll have to keep a diary though - write everything down. The funny anecdotes and stuff..."

"Yeah, but what's the angle?" I said hesitantly. I was already thinking about the heat and long hours, and how I'd be throwing myself back into the furnace again – coping with it all in a strange language. I just hoped I wouldn't be working for another nutter like Grant.

Boris was still talking...

"It's brilliant! Take a year off, scuttle down to San Sebastian in an old jalopy and learn the trade. I just wish I could do it myself, but what with the mortgage and the bloody kids...I can't be on the breadline again, you know that. But you're alright – you haven't got any!"

"I've still got a massive amount to learn," I said.

"You'll be marvellous – just bring the kitchen to life for all those arm-chair chefs out there. Just the basics on what you need to learn to become a professional cook. Improve your dinner parties no end!

"You know...knife skills, different vegetable cuts, knowing the difference between brunoise and julienne. Prepping meat, veg and fish, knowing how to portion and store food, stock control, that sort of thing."

He took another swig of wine and topped himself up. I still wasn't sure if the lunch was on him.

"Garnishes - making dishes look nice. Making pastry and dough, what to look for when buying food from the market. Has the fish got bright eyes and red gills? If not, why not!"

"Why not?"

"It's all got to be in there, you know! Fill it with cooking techniques, recipes, and pad out the rest with anecdotes. You know the stuff. And you've got the passion for it!"

The last was his trump card, and we both knew it. He had the same romantic view of the kitchen I had. He'd worked as a chef for ten years in Paris and London before he got too tired and took an easy job sitting behind a desk all day, writing about food, and making occasional forays to the pass.

He wrote restaurant reviews from the kitchen – that way, he said, you could try everything going out, not just what you ordered, and got a fairer view of the menu. And, of course, he could stuff himself with more food that way.

I've often wondered whether there is any real difference between a foodie and a glutton. People will tell you foodies care about the provenance and quality of the food they eat,

75

but gluttons will eat anything. But I'm not so sure. I've eaten many dirty kebabs with chefs and restaurant managers whose seasonal, animal barcode menus read like a hymn sheet to River Cottage. But to be fair, it's what you savour after a night cooking or serving rich restaurant food.

Boris broke open another claw and began reminiscing about his days working in kitchens in France.

"I burned everything old bean. Everything!"

His eyes glittered with passion, too much wine, and the wetness of longing regret as he told me about the smoke and the heat, the shameful, napkin-concealed ortolan feasts, and the thousands of pounds of caviar and foie gras he'd shovelled down his throat.

"But first we'll have to get your knife skills properly up to speed. Can't have you rocketing off to Spain, cutting off fingers! Otherwise it'll be a very short book indeed!"

And that was it. Boris said he'd phone the publishers to arrange a meeting, and make a few calls to kitchens to get me some work experience. And I was left with the bill. I sat there for an hour wondering about the possibilities while the waiters brushed breadcrumbs from the tables around me.

Occasionally, one of the chefs would stand in the doorway, puffing blue smoke and getting a rare glimpse of sunshine. I wanted to be that chef, basking in those precious few moments. I didn't want to just write about food, and stand on the sidelines reviewing restaurants. I wanted to cook for a living. But at least this way I'd be able to do both. The possibilities were endless, and for the first time in a long time I felt like I was truly on the right road – even if it was in an old banger that probably wouldn't get as far as Calais.

BORIS PHONED to say he'd arranged for me to do three days at The Dorchester Hotel so I could learn a few skills before leaving the country. I got a Tube to Park Lane, and met Eric, the executive chef, at 10am. He took me into his office, and we chatted about the hotel kitchens and how they were run. It was far more relaxed than I'd been expecting. I thought he'd probe me to find out what I was really doing there, and whether I was writing an expose on the place. But he didn't seem bothered in the slightest.

"So you know Boris..." he began. "He's a fat bastard isn't he!"

Eric had a pretty good sense of humour for a German. He asked about my cooking experience, and laughed when I told him about the book idea. Then he introduced me to his executive sous chef Rudi, who took me to the changing room and handed me a starched set of whites, emblazoned with the hotel's name. He even had to show me how to fasten the buttons.

I was then sent to work with Wayne, a surly commis chef with a fat tongue, and more than a passing resemblance to Jamie Oliver. He even used the word "pukka" from time to time. He showed me the lobster tank, and pulled out two of the creatures and held them next to each other, hoping they would fight.

Our first job was opening and cleaning scallops. They were massive things and seemed even bigger than the one I'd found in Brittany all those years ago. He told me they were diver-caught and cost well over a pound each. But I couldn't get to grips with them, and after mangling a few, one of the sous chefs spotted my pitiful efforts and told me to watch Wayne do the rest.

Wayne boasted that he was one of the quickest shuckers there – and could even hold his own with the blindingly-fast Chinese chefs in The Dorchester's Oriental Kitchen. He held each scallop curved-side down at eye-level, and then twisted the shell open with a spoon. I'd always used a knife before, but he said a spoon causes less damage to the shell, and makes it easier to pop open.

Then he got a palette knife and ran it tight against the top shell through the ligament holding the muscle meat. He said if you cut off the flesh cleanly enough, you could see the pattern of the shell when you fried them.

He threw away the sandy frill, and kept the white meat and orange coral. He washed them a number of times to remove any sand and then drained them. He said that most restaurants only serve the white meat, but the coral was brilliant for making scallop dust. You dry them on the bottom shelf in a cool oven, and blitz them into dust in a grinder. He said it was good for seasoning scallops because it helped with the caramelisation process and colour.

After a few minutes, he asked me what I was doing there, and I told him about the book, and said I was sharpening my knife skills before going to work in Spain.

"Can you speak Spanish?" he asked.

I shook my head.

"Well, you really will be fucked then."

It was another taste of the huge learning curve in front of me – and it was even harder to stomach from a 19-year-old. I'd need Sherpas where I was going.

For lunch service, I worked with an Irish chef called Paul. He was terrified because it was the first time he'd been trusted to cook The Dorchester's famed table-carved roast beef.

"If it's wrong, it's not like you can just cook another. It's got to be right first time."

They served two beef joints – a large, medium-rare rib of Aberdeen Angus, and a smaller sirloin for those who liked their meat cremated. About 20 minutes before service, Paul took the joints out of the oven, so they could rest. He squeezed each joint with his fingers to test them. He said the firmness told you how well cooked the meat was, and you could test this by pushing your thumb against each finger on your left hand to form a circle, and feeling the tightness in the pad between your thumb and index finger as you did so.

The tautness between thumb and little finger was similar to squeezing well-done meat, thumb and ring finger medium, thumb and middle finger medium rare, and thumb and index finger rare.

Paul melted butter in a pan and threw in a sprig of rosemary and a crushed garlic clove and poured it over the beef. It gave the meat a lovely aroma and glossy finish. He then placed the joints on a table under bright lights in the centre of the kitchen. It was quite a ceremony watching the meat being examined by Eric as the other cooks looked on.

An ancient waiter, who ran the beef carving trolleys in The Grill room, called over.

"Which one's which?" he said.

Paul went bright red, and then realised it was a joke, and tried to laugh it off.

"He's been here donkey's years," he said to me. "His eyesight's no good."

For the next two days, I was kept safely out of harm's reach in the Italian kitchen, helping the chefs vac-pack lobster in olive oil, garlic and rosemary for the spaghetti dish, and pin-boning red mullet. I was also taught how to make squid ink pasta and focaccia. On the last day, I helped Rudi dress 500 Caesar

79

salads for a banquet as waiters queued impatiently for their plates.

The whole experience overwhelmed me. But I had learned a few techniques. Boris phoned and asked how I'd got on. He was clearly excited and went through everything I'd been taught. I tried my best to sound positive.

"It'll come," he said. "You won't learn it all overnight. It took me years and I was still useless at the end!"

He had arranged for me to do a week at Petrus, under the watchful gaze of Gordon Ramsay's then lieutenant, Marcus Wareing. I'd heard it was one of the toughest kitchens in London, and wasn't looking forward to it in the slightest. I also had serious doubts about how much I would learn as a bumbling amateur working in a Premier League kitchen. If it was anything like The Dorchester, then I'd be thoroughly out of my depth and would probably only be trusted peeling spuds.

But I was saved when I drove past a Spanish fish restaurant I'd eaten in a couple of times and saw a sandwich board outside saying 'kitchen help wanted'. I thought that if I got the job, I'd be able to pick up some Spanish cooking skills for my trip, and maybe learn a bit of the language at the same time.

Vieira was a 17th century pub with a huge car park in south-west London. Inside, the tables were packed so tightly together you could hardly get a cigarette paper between them. The food was reasonable but simple, and the prices just shy of expensive. The whole operation was about maximising profit, and I soon learned there was a lot more to running a successful kitchen than knowing how to cook.

I parked the car and strolled up to the front door. The place was closed. Suddenly a huge poodle jumped up at the glass, barking ferociously. I stood there for a minute, and was about to wander round the back, when a small, bespectacled man in his 70s pulled back a curtain and studied me. From the initial look on his face, he probably thought I was a tax inspector. He held back the slavering poodle and opened the door. He was immaculately dressed in a white flannel shirt and trousers, and shook my hand warmly.

There was no interview for the job. Miguel sat me down in the dining room, and didn't even ask what work I'd done before. On hearing I wanted to be a chef, he looked at me blankly, and then delivered his thoughts like a High Court judge.

It was probably the most honest summing up of the catering trade I've ever heard. Forget all that testosterone-filled tosh from young thrusters wanting to be the next big thing, or the nonsense they spout on reality TV cooking shows – professional cooking isn't a divine calling, it's just a job like any other.

Miguel sipped an espresso through a straw, and his short arms began gesticulating. My throat was as dry as Gandhi's sandal, but he didn't offer me a drink.

"Do you know how long I've been a chef for?"

I shrugged. I'd never been much good with ages.

"For 50 years! And I can say that through it all, even now, you have good days and bad days, it doesn't matter how much you know.

"For me, the good days are when I go and speak to a customer at the end of the night, and they say 'you know Miguel that was a beautiful piece of fish!' That gives me a good feeling. But you know, catering's a hard business, one of the hardest, and the bad days, well..."

His eyes floated to the ceiling, and then turned back to me as though he had said too much. He asked me a few questions, but didn't press me on my cooking experience, or why I wanted to be a chef. He just said it was impossible to get kitchen staff.

He spoke about how important it was to go to catering college and learn textbook techniques like beurre manie, sabayon, trussing, kneading, barding, and proving et al. He even said I could work there on a placement while I was studying for my NVQ. But deep down, I think he was just sizing me up, wondering how long my passion would last once the realities of the job had kicked in.

He said that in his younger days, he'd had seven chefs working for him. He was climbing the AA rosette ladder, nearing his first Michelin star, but he'd soon got wise to the stress and financial pressure that brings. He said he was solely in it for the money, and that was the only reason to run a restaurant.

"Stars don't pay the gas bill. It's just bums on seats that matter. Doesn't matter how good your fish is – if you can't pay the rent, it'll be rotting in the fridge, and then even the cats won't eat it."

He took another sip of coffee, his eyes sparkling like buttons.

"You know Lennie, when I came to this country I had £5 in my pocket and couldn't speak any English – just a few words. I turned up in Essex and got a job in a fish and chip shop near the beach. And you know the accents they have there!"

He puffed out his cheeks, and laughed.

"I could barely speak a word, and it was 'ketchup with this mate', 'vinegar with that one', I had to learn fast you know! We did 500 cod and chips every lunch – 500 cod!

"And then slowly I learned to cook. Each job – pub, restaurant, fast food, whatever - I learned something new. I've been in this business 50 years and I can tell you, I've seen everything! Arguments between chefs - fights! We had to break up knife fights using saucepan lids to protect us!"

He paused and expected me to be shocked. After working at the bistro, I knew how all manner of madness could take over during service. It's all to do with the heat, stress and the proximity of knives. He finished off by saying I could learn a lot at Vieira, and that 99% of the food was home-made.

"We even make our own mayonnaise," he said proudly.

The menu on the chalkboard certainly sounded impressive. But after a week, it was obvious most of the food was bought-in. The lobster bisque came out of a tin and was doctored with wine and cream to make it 'home-made', and the gravy for the calves' liver and onion dish was made from Bisto.

I WORKED from 10am to 2pm five days a week, and was paid £5 an hour in cash. I'd then change out of my chef whites into a suit and work at the paper most evenings. I knew how ludicrous those hours were to a chef, but I couldn't pay the rent on the restaurant wages alone. And Miguel was only offering part-time work.

The old Spaniard ran front-of-house, and would do the cooking when his stressed, obnoxious son Fabio took his annual two-week holiday or had a rare day off. Fabio was a stocky, hairy man with tufts of chest hair poking up from his whites.

Whereas his father was the epitome of grace and affected English charm - a man who kept notes about his customers in a tiny Moleskin book so he could join in their conversations with a wry comment - Fabio had the charisma of a dung beetle. That was the reason he was kept tucked away in the kitchen. All his father could say about him was he was a "good grafter".

Mr and Mrs Henry, as they were known, did 90% of the work in the kitchen. They were a Romanian couple who arrived at work each day at 9am. In the mornings, while Mrs Henry peeled and sliced hundreds of spuds, scaled fish, and made soup, her husband cleaned the fryers and stoves, and prepped the rest of the veg.

I'd never seen such a clean kitchen before – the place sparkled. They changed the oil in the fryers every day, whereas in some places it is changed once a month at best, and the oil looks like dark treacle with black jetsam. Poke around in most professional kitchens, and you'll find grime in any corner difficult to get a mop into, but there was none at Vieira. Or at least none that Fabio could find, and he made it his business to catch them out.

The Romanians worked solidly until 3pm, and then drove eight miles home for a quick nap, before arriving back at 5.30pm. They would be lucky to get out by midnight, and sometimes this stretched to well past 1am. When they were really behind, they would take buckets of potatoes back with them to peel in the small hours.

They had one day off a week, when they would hunt through charity shops or car boot sales for bargains, and send them back to Romania. They said they had a farmhouse in the north of the country, filled with unopened boxes of goods. They constantly moaned about their lot and their £3 an hour wages, and I didn't blame them. It appeared the minimum wage laws stretched no further than the doorstep, and I'm sure Miguel only paid me £5 an hour because I was British.

Mr and Mrs Henry's lives were ruled by fear – and that came in the shape of Miguel's second wife Manuela, a tanned, stoat-like woman with dyed orange hair and far too much blue eye shadow. She was a constant source of friction, and would wander downstairs from time to time and shout at the Romanians in Spanish.

The couple were even too scared to eat anything in case they got caught. Once Fabio had opened Mrs Henry's mouth and discovered her munching a carrot. He'd joked that it would come out of her wages, but like all his jokes it was cruel and thin.

Although Mr and Mrs Henry were confident, intelligent people, they had been broken down over the years by Manuela and Fabio. In their previous lives, Mrs Henry had been a medical researcher at a university, and her husband a manager at a railway station, with 60 people under him. But the money Miguel paid was more than they could get at home. They said their daughter had leukaemia, and they needed the cash to pay for her medical bills, and that was the only reason they put up with life at the restaurant.

I felt sorry for them as they peeled endless bags of spuds. They told me when they'd first got there, life was much easier because they'd used a potato peeling machine outside in the yard. But that had stopped when Manuela burst into the kitchen one day, complaining about the noise. The machine was still there, propped up against the wall where the dog slept. The sight of it must have driven them mad with rage.

The front-of-house workers were mostly Romanian too. Apparently, Miguel had a contact in the country who found him good workers. He used Romanians because the language was similar to Spanish, and his wife had never bothered to learn English, and he could pay them a pittance.

The restaurant manager was a Romanian called Sabina. She was a short, stocky woman with a spray-on smile. She had a 12-year-old son, who she claimed was a genius.

I made a blunder in my first week and our relationship was never the same again. In a quiet moment, Sabina asked me to guess her age. Normally when a woman asks, I say 21 even if she doesn't have her own teeth. But it didn't work on her, and she kept asking me to guess, so figuring she was at least in her late 40s, I knocked off ten years and said 38. The room went deathly quiet.

"I'm 31!" she wailed, her eyes darting at me like angry wasps. "Maybe I've had a harder life than women in your country!"

I didn't doubt that for a second.

MOST OF the cleaning was done by the time I strolled in at 10am – it was a completely unrealistic taste of kitchen life, and I loved every second of it. I'd spend the first two hours doing the easier prep jobs – making crepes, cutting carrots into batons, chopping up parsley etc. None of it was particularly demanding, and after a while I started asking for more taxing tasks.

Every few days I'd make a new batch of mayonnaise. Miguel was very particular about how I made it, and guided me carefully through the first two batches to make sure it didn't split. It was that beautiful pale yellow sort I'd always associated with summers in France and Spain.

He'd tell me to take the eggs out of the fridge an hour before I made it, then break four egg yolks into a soup bowl containing a tablespoon of English mustard and set it aside for ten minutes. Then I'd break one whole egg into a mixing bowl and beat it with an electric hand whisk, on its lowest setting. I'd add the yolks, a teaspoon of paprika, and seasoning, and slowly trickle in one-and-a-half pints of vegetable oil until I had a thick, glossy emulsion.

Miguel said that by adding ingredients like anchovies, garlic, tarragon and orange juice you could then make sauces like remoulade or maltaise. But we only used tartare sauce for fish, and marie-rose for crab and prawn cocktails and smoked salmon cornucopias. For cost reasons, Miguel never used capers, and we made the tartare by adding diced gherkins,

86

Spanish onion, spring onion, chives and hard-boiled egg yolks to the mayonnaise. For the marie-rose, we'd add tomato ketchup, Worcester sauce, cheap brandy, parsley, and a dash of Tabasco.

I ran the starters section during lunch service. The menu was huge. There were 25 starters on a la carte – including grilled gambas al ajillo, deep-fried king prawns, whitebait, king prawns thermidor, grilled scallops and bacon, deep-fried camembert, melon and Parma ham, calamares a la Romana, prawn and mushroom crepes, grilled goat's cheese and basil salad, and hot smoked mackerel fillets.

But most people ordered the two-course lunch menu for £10, and skipped dessert. So mostly I just deep-fried whitebait, and king prawns in Japanese breadcrumbs. They came frozen in boxes and all I had to do was bung them in the fryer for a couple of minutes until they were golden. The hardest part was knowing how many whitebait to serve. Too big a handful, and Fabio's eyes were on me like a hawk. Too few and it just looked ridiculous.

One couple, who had spent years working in Tokyo, said the king prawns were the best Japanese food they'd ever had. They must have eaten in McDonald's every day while they were there. It just shows there is no accounting for taste, and all food is massively subjective.

We had a simple system for the starter plates. Mr Henry was head of salads, and he'd line them up for me as the orders came in. It was easy to tell which was which. The whitebait came with a few shreds of iceberg lettuce, whereas the Japanese prawns had a couple of slices of tomato as well. There was extra luxury for the more expensive grilled goat's cheese and smoked mackerel dishes – maybe even a few leaves of frisee and some cucumber.

And then there was the obligatory lemon wedge. It was Mr Henry's job to cut them up, and Fabio would scold him for only getting six wedges out of each lemon, instead of eight. Every part of the cooking operation was run on miserly, mealy-mouthed efficiency - right down to using the potato water for the mash and not milk.

Fabio was horrified on the first day, when he spotted me chucking in half a pack of butter and a tub of double cream as I'd been taught at the bistro. He was so appalled by the extravagance he could scarcely get the words out.

For some reason, it reminded me of a Floyd episode when a youthful-looking Marco Pierre White shows him how they make pomme puree at Harveys – hot, boiled potatoes straight into the Robot Coupe, a tonne of softened butter, and enough hot milk to turn it into a thick custard. That sort of cooking seemed a country mile away from Vieira's.

Cream was rarely used in the kitchen, for cost reasons, and nearly all the sauces were thickened with flour. Miguel said there were three tricks to making a good roux-based sauce – always use a whisk, always whisk in hot liquid, and always sieve the sauce to get rid of any lumps. He showed me how to make the fish veloute he used for most of the sauce-based dishes, from the fillets of sole bonne femme to the prawn and mushroom crepes.

You make fish stock from the bones, heads and trimmings left over from the sole, turbot and bass fillets. Then you melt a knob of margarine in a pan over a low heat, and stir in the same amount of flour, and gently cook the paste over a low flame until you have a golden-brown roux. You heat some fish stock and a little semi-skimmed milk in a separate pan, and slowly whisk in small amounts of the liquid, waiting until it is all dissolved before adding the next batch.

You then simmer it gently for 20 minutes, stirring constantly, until it is reduced by a third. After that, you sieve and store it in old ice cream tubs next to the sofrito (basic Spanish tomato sauce) in the walk-in chiller.

For the sofrito, I'd chop up four large Spanish onions, and slice ten garlic cloves, and fry them gently in olive oil for five minutes. Then I'd add salt and pepper, a kilo of quartered plum tomatoes, and a kilo of quartered and cored red peppers. I'd simmer the vegetables for an hour before adding a pint of water. I'd then liquidise and sieve the sauce. We served the sauce with grilled scallops, and as a base for the fish soup.

I PREPPED hundreds of mussels a day, washing them in the sink, pulling off the beards, and discarding any that were cracked. Fabio hated waste, and would check the mussels I threw away. If any were open, he'd squeeze them a few times to see if they would close. If they didn't, it meant they were dead – and even Fabio accepted they couldn't be served. Then I'd scrape off the barnacles with a blunt knife, and rub the shells with a scouring pad so they shone like black pearls.

Although miserliness was endemic, and we used the cheapest wine Miguel could get his hands on at the cash and carry, the mussels were delicious and one of the most popular meals on a la carte. You melt a knob of butter in a pan, and fry chopped parsley stalks, garlic and spring onion greens for a minute. After that, you add an equal amount of white wine and fish veloute and bring the liquid to the boil before tossing in the mussels, covering the pan, and cooking them for a couple of minutes until they open.

Despite their initial hostility, I grew reasonably close to Mr and Mrs Henry as the weeks went by, and was invited for a meal one evening. They lived in a dingy, brown-wallpapered flat above an Asian grocery store. They told me how proud they were that an Englishman had come round to see them.

They gave me beer and kabanos sausages, and spent the night bitching about their dreary lives at the restaurant.

Mr Henry polished off a bottle of rum, and began waving a knife around inches from my face, telling me about how he'd like to "kill Fabio like a fish".

WHENEVER MIGUEL, Fabio and Manuela were out of earshot, Mrs Henry's ham-like face would crease into a grimace and she would scold me for not getting a "proper job".

"You are English, why do you work here?" she'd say, holding up her beefy forearms and dancing the words between her fingers. "We can't! Me and Henry have to work here, but you are English - you can get any job. If you were my son, I would punch you!"

"I like cooking," I'd always answer.

"What because it's romantic?" she'd spit. "You only work mornings - you wouldn't like it if you worked the same hours as us. Me and Henry...we get sick with the work..."

Her cartoon eyes were so emphatic, she reminded me of a pantomime dame. She'd then moan about how hard their lives were, cooking and cleaning under the repressive, poisonous smog of Manuela's spite.

Mrs Henry told me she heard the ticker machine that sent the orders into the kitchen in her sleep. It made a rasping, metallic sound like someone sharpening a knife.

"You hear the machine in your sleep?"

"No," I said.

"You wait until you do! Then you won't want to work in a kitchen! Whenever I hear that sound it cuts me."

She ran a finger knife-like across her throat – the same way she did when she talked about what she'd like to do to Manuela.

If I picked up a mop to help them clean, she'd chide me.

"So you like cooking? You want to learn technique? Learn about a mop! Why do you want to work in a place like this? You should work anywhere but this!"

Her words had little impact. I was only working four hours a day and loving every minute of it. I didn't even have to clean down after service. Once when I stayed behind to help, Mr Henry jabbed at me.

"You're the only man I know who likes cooking! Maybe you make a good wife!"

He grabbed my arm and tried to waltz.

"Maybe you like men!" he said.

The only way I could get Mrs Henry off my back was to tell her I was learning the trade so I could set up my own restaurant. At that point she'd become very interested.

"Well, if you're going to do that, you should do that now," she'd say. "I'll teach you what you need to know. Me and Henry can help you."

Other times, she nagged me about being single. She threatened to fix me up with a "good Romanian woman" - maybe even her daughter.

"She is a lawyer. She earns good money. All she needs is an introduction to come here to England. Or you meet her when you come to Romania – that's if you do want to come and see us..."

We'd spend hours planning the restaurant we'd run in her country. Apparently, if you knew the right people, and Mr and Mrs Henry knew the right people, you could buy a hotel in the mountains for less than £100,000.

Sabina also found out I was single, and made it her mission to find me a woman.

"You don't want an English girl," she'd say. "All they do is get drunk – I've seen them in the high street! Romanian woman aren't like that."

One day she brought in a photo of a young woman she said was her cousin and showed it to me in the bar when no-one else was around. She put her finger to her lips, and told me I shouldn't tell anyone, especially Mrs Henry. The girl had long black hair, a chalky-white face, and a just-got-out-of-a-coffin look.

"She cannot get a visa to come to this country. All she needs is an introduction," she sighed. "I'm sad because there's nothing I can do for her. If I could only get her to this country her life would be okay..."

THE ATMOSPHERE would quickly worsen whenever Manuela burst into the kitchen. She was supposed to help out during service, but did little more than get in the way. Her speciality was frying the calves' liver and onions, making the fish soup, and cooking the paella. Occasionally, she would blunder into my section and cause chaos.

One day there was a little more backchat than normal, and she had a row with Fabio outside in the yard. It was in Spanish, but I could pick up a few words. I could tell she was questioning his manhood and criticising him for not running the kitchen with an iron fist.

Fabio returned just as Mr Henry cut a slice from the goat's cheese log and handed it to me to be grilled. The slice was slightly wonky and crumbly. I was pouring the dried basil on when Fabio snatched it out of my hand.

"What the fuck is that!" he screamed. The fury seemed to come out of nowhere. "You can't even cut a piece of cheese straight! I tell you to do things and you don't do them! You can't even cut cheese! Look at that!"

Mr Henry looked shocked, and then angry.

"It's Mr Henry do this, Mr Henry do that. I am not a machine!" he shouted back.

"I'm not paying you to be a machine! I ask you to do a simple task and you can't even do that! Why the fuck can't you cut cheese straight?"

Mrs Henry looked flustered and near to tears. She shouted a few words in Romanian at her husband, but he waved her away.

"I am good worker. The reason you shout at me is because you don't like me. You don't like Mr Henry! I am not the one who makes mistakes!"

It was obvious who he was referring to. The argument raged on for a couple of minutes, until Mrs Henry managed to calm her husband.

I saw Manuela looking round slyly from the desserts section. It was the only time I ever saw her smile. She traipsed in later as though nothing had happened.

Generally Manuela ignored me. I only got on the wrong side of her once - when I put on a red apron instead of a blue one. Fabio was brought in to translate the bollocking - the red ones were for the pot wash, the blue ones for the cooks. I don't know why it upset her so much. Perhaps she thought I'd done it deliberately to annoy her.

93

She didn't speak to me for a couple of days after that. And then Miguel must have had a word with her, because she called me over one morning and showed me how to make her paella. Customers would have to give 24 hours' notice for the dish, and some ordered it for dinner parties and weddings.

Miguel said there was a lot of nonsense spoken about using the right type of rice, and his wife would just use the cheap, easy-cook variety. I'd never been a big fan of paella, but her secret ingredient was freshly-squeezed lemon juice, and it really gave the dish a delicious taste.

She finely chopped a large Spanish onion, a red pepper, and four cloves of garlic, and fried them in olive oil for ten minutes in a paella pan. She sliced four cleaned squid into thin rings, and skinned and chopped three large tomatoes, and added them to the pan, and let it simmer for 20 minutes. Meanwhile, she chopped up three chicken legs, coated the pieces in seasoned flour, and deep-fried them until they were almost cooked through.

She then mixed in the chicken and simmered the pan for another ten minutes. Then she added a handful of green olives, two big cups of rice and water. She stirred the paella for another ten minutes until the rice was just cooked, and then added salt and half a cup of freshly-squeezed lemon juice.

She scaled and gutted a sea bream, removed the head and tail, and chopped the body into six steaks. She coated the pieces in seasoned flour and deep-fried them for three minutes before grilling six gambas and six green-lipped mussels. She'd then decorate the paella dish with the seafood, and put it on the table and let the customers serve themselves.

The next day, Manuela showed me how to make her Seville marmalade pudding. She buttered the bottom and sides of a pudding dish with margarine, and then spread 25 slices of bread with margarine and Seville marmalade, and cut them into diagonal halves. She arranged them in the dish so there were no gaps, and sprinkled raisins over each layer.

She made the custard by whisking two whole eggs and four yolks with 4oz of caster sugar and a few drops of vanilla essence. She then heated a pint of milk until it was body temperature, and slowly whisked it into the eggs over a pan of boiling water. She poured the custard over the bread slices, covered the dish with foil, and baked it in the oven at 160C for one hour.

AFTER FOUR months, it became my job to scale, gut, skin and trim the fish that arrived every Tuesday and Friday mornings from Billingsgate Market. Miguel warned me how easy it was to prick yourself on the bass and bream spines, and showed me how to hold each fish delicately between thumb and forefinger to avoid bruising the flesh.

I was taking no chances. I remembered a story from The Dorchester about a chef who'd jabbed his thumb on a bass spine, and had his arm in a sling for three weeks when it turned an ugly green.

The old Spaniard told me how important it was to gut the fish as soon as they arrived to stop them tainting the flesh. He also scaled them straight away, saying they were much easier to get off when the fish was fresh.

We stood at the pot wash's sink, the water splashing, as we snipped off the fins with scissors. Then he showed me how to scale them, scraping the fish against the grain from tail to head with a metal descaler he'd brought back from his last trip to Spain. He said when he was a boy growing up in Valencia, they'd used the serrated edge of a scallop shell.

"You must be thorough - the customers complain if they find a scale," he said as we peppered our whites with flying silver.

He held up a bass and kissed it, showing me how it had all the hallmarks of a "beautiful fresh fish" - its eyes were clear and bright, its gills bright red, and its flesh firm to the touch.

"These are easy because they are farmed," he said. "They have a much harder life when they're wild - the scales are thicker, and they're not so fat. These had an easy life - no big fish, no problems over food - the fishermen just throw them squid each day!"

He washed the bass and bream again and slit open the belly. He put his hand in, twisting slightly, and pulled out the entrails. The bottom of the sink was soon filled with pink, yellow, and red guts, and half-digested pieces of squid. It was amazing how much some of them had eaten.

He then removed the gills - snipping the area where they joined the head and mouth - and scraped away the black blood with a teaspoon until the backbone was smooth and clean.

For service, we'd slash them three or four times on each side, brush them with vegetable oil, and grill them for ten minutes until they were charred and bitter on the outside and succulently moist in the middle. No salt or pepper, just a knob of herb butter melted over the fish. It was simplicity in the extreme, but his elderly customers liked it that way.

We used different butters for different fish. I'd soften the butter near the oven and mix in finely chopped basil, watercress, thyme, garlic, parsley, anchovy, or red pepper, and season to taste. Then I'd wrap the mixture in foil, roll it into a sausage shape, and cut it into rounds and store it in the chiller.

Miguel also showed me how to prep the Dover soles. These were his favourite and he spoke of them grandly, telling me how the Romans had prized them above all other fish, and called them solea Jovi (Jupiter's sandal). I suppose with their oval shape, and leathery skin they did look a bit like sandals.

He said the best Dovers came from the deepest trenches in the English Channel, and had a far sweeter taste than lemon sole – which he said were not soles anyway, but members of the dab family.

Miguel trimmed the spiny side fins with scissors, and snipped off the tail. He put the fish dark-side up on a board, and with his thumb, gently loosened the skin on each side, moving from tail to head. He then grasped the flap at one corner of the tail and ripped the skin off like a plaster, holding the delicate flesh with the other hand to stop it tearing. He turned the fish over and did the same with the white side. The skinned, anaemic-looking fish were piled up in trays in the fridge. When ordered, they were oiled and grilled and served whole with a pat of thyme butter.

When I wasn't working at the paper, I'd practise my knife skills and read cookery books in the evenings. One day I asked Miguel about trying out some classic sole recipes like filets de sole Cubat, where the fish was smeared with mushroom duxelles and browned in the oven with mornay sauce. I tried to appeal to his stingy nature by saying we could just chuck some cheddar in the veloute for the mornay sauce.

But he said his customers just wanted plainly-cooked fish that tasted of the sea. When I suggested sole aux legumes poeles, saying it couldn't be simpler because it was just pan-fried vegetables and chopped parsley, he shook his head and smiled, and said there was no finer recipe in the world than sole meuniere with a few drops of lemon.

MIGUEL NEVER varied his menu, and the same side vegetables went out with each order – sauté potatoes, carrot batons, peas, and courgette wedges in batter. It was basic but effective. But then it had to be - there were only four chefs serving up to 150 covers.

Some of the world's best eateries have five times that number serving just 30 customers, which is why so many of them haemorrhage cash. But not at Miguel's. Far from it. Everything was streamlined, and I learned a huge amount from him. And although I didn't like the way his family treated the Romanians, I grew fond of the old Spaniard. He was a terrible miser, but he had a lot more heart than the rest of them.

His gross profit on some dishes was staggering. Most restaurants aim for a 30% food cost on each dish – but some of Miguel's must have been a fraction of that. The French onion soup Mrs Henry made cost peanuts to make. All she did was stew slices of Spanish onion over a low heat until they were transparent, add some salt and pepper and paprika, and pour in a couple of pints of Bisto gravy. Then she'd put grated red Leicester cheese on a French bread crouton, float it on top, and put the soup bowl under the grill until the cheese melted.

Mrs Henry was intensely proud of her soup, and it was strangely moreish. Once when she was off, and Manuela made it in her absence, some of the customers complained that the soup wasn't the same as normal. Mrs Henry would repeat the story with relish. She also told how a couple from France had come in one day and said it was the best French onion soup they'd tasted. I had difficulty believing that one.

Miguel would hide the Bisto tub upstairs in his living quarters. Whenever you needed it, you'd have to ask him to bring it down, and as soon as you'd finished he'd smuggle it back up there. The Romanians made jokes about how tight he was, and how much Bisto cost. But for once, it wasn't about the margin. It was just that he didn't want customers knowing he used gravy granules.

Once, an American tourist peered through the serving hatch and asked me what the gravy was made from. I answered, but had clearly stepped over some unseen boundary, and Fabio scowled at me for the rest of service. Afterwards, he called me over and asked what I'd said.

"Beef stock," I replied.

"That's alright then," he sneered.

I'd been there six months when Miguel started showing people round the kitchen. There was whispered talk among the Romanians that he was selling the place. Despite their constant whingeing and misery, they were genuinely shocked that they might soon be out of a job. They were angry that Miguel hadn't told them he was selling up, and I was angry too. Most of the prospective buyers were Asian families. I thought the last thing the area needed was another Indian restaurant.

I went home and did property searches on the internet. In the end, I found Vieira for sale on a website. There was no name, all it said was "prominent restaurant near Kingston". But I recognised the pictures of the kitchen and dining room. I phoned up and pretended to be a buyer, and the agent confirmed it was Vieira before saying I'd need to fill out a confidentiality contract. Miguel was selling the freehold for £2.5 million, but two weeks later the price had dropped by £400,000.

I TYPED out a cheffing CV, showing the limited experience I'd got, and scanned trade rags and the internet for work. One advert in The Caterer and Hotelkeeper magazine caught my eye. A staff agency was looking for chefs in Cornwall. I imagined myself at a beachfront restaurant, finishing my shifts with a few beers on the cliff-top, listening to the crash of the waves below.

I thought with the fish prepping skills I'd learned, I could probably get work at a seafood restaurant. I phoned up the agency boss, and he told me they were looking for a commis chef at a luxury hotel near Penzance. He said the hotel was overlooking the sea. I could smell the salt in the breeze, and hear the screech of the gulls.

I went back to Vieira for what would be my last day. I gutted and trimmed the fish waiting for me in the sink, and then Fabio told me to make the crumble. I cored and peeled about 50 cooking apples, and cut them into segments. Fabio was very particular about crumble. He liked whole pieces of apple in there so you'd only poach them for a minute before refreshing them under the cold tap.

I put the apple segments in a pan with a splash of water, and was about to clean down my board and start on the crumble mix when Mrs Henry started chatting about a programme she'd seen the night before on UFOs.

She knew I was a sucker for unexplained mysteries, and after a few seconds I was gripped, listening to her story about how a Romanian MiG-21's onboard camera had captured four unknown objects smashing its cockpit as it flew over Transylvania. As soon as there was a second of silence, she filled it quickly, her mind racing to the next story.

Mr Henry walked past from time to time, nodding enthusiastically as we talked. A few moments later, a bitter smell drifted over from the stove, and I suddenly remembered the apples. They'd turned to a brown mush, and some were welded to the bottom of the pan.

Mrs Henry skipped over innocently, a concerned look in her eyes.

"Quick, don't show Fabio!" she said loudly.

"Show him what?"

Fabio walked over and stuck his nose over the pot.

"It's a fucking puree!" he yelled.

He made continual jibes about the apples for the rest of service. Mrs Henry caught my eye from time to time and gave me a sympathetic look. I realised the Romanians hadn't been bothered about me wasting my life as a chef after all - they just didn't want me stealing their jobs. I was proud they saw me as a threat, and imagined them sitting in their flat, swigging rum and planning the whole thing the night before. If they'd gone to that much trouble, I must be a half-decent cook after all, I thought.

Miguel phoned up from time to time, but I never answered.

"We're worried about you Lennie," he'd say. His voice messages became more frantic, but I think he was just worried about how they'd cope in the run-up to Christmas.

I often wonder what he's doing now, and always picture him sitting in the sun on the terrace of his mansion in Spain, sipping a sickly-sweet espresso through a straw, and reflecting on his five decades of hard work. I knew he had done it the clever way. He laughed at the notion that chefs are pseudo-Bohemian artists, battling a maelstrom of emotions within. It was profitability that was important, not chasing awards and media profiles.

His empire had grown from a fiver, through a string of leasehold pubs and restaurants, to a mortgage-free eatery in an expensive part of London. Over the years he'd taken suitcases of cash back to Spain, and bought dozens of properties. Mrs Henry claimed the Spanish were all descended from pirates, and it was in their blood to loot and pillage. She might have been right about Miguel though. He'd certainly found treasure on foreign shores.

101

CHAPTER SIX

Ian, the agency boss, phoned to confirm the interview at the hotel was going ahead and I could stay at the head chef's house on the Monday night, and do the trial on the Tuesday. He said I'd need whites and a set of knives. I'd only got two knives - a Henckels chef's knife and a paring knife – and had always been supplied with whites before.

I drove up to Dennys in Soho and bought five second-hand chef's jackets, two pairs of second-hand checked trousers, two new white hats, and a pair of steel-capped lace-ups. They were the most expensive shoes in the shop, but the South African shop assistant said I'd need them.

"You're going to be spending so long on your bloody feet mate, you might as well have good shoes," she said.

I had enough cash for a set of Global knives as well, but I thought my two German blades would do for the time being, and I'd need every penny of savings to subsidise my pay. If I passed the trial, it would be my first full-time cheffing job. I was 41-years-old and about to leave the celebrity-obsessed Fleet Street circus to lock myself in the padded asylum of professional cooking.

I plucked up enough courage and gave up my job. I don't know where the last badly-formed quenelle of impetus came from, but I went into work one day and asked to have a word with the editor. He told me he was busy and could I come back in ten minutes. It was a long ten minutes. I smoked a cigarette and didn't sway and kept my nerve and handed in my notice.

He looked surprised and quite pleased.

"I've been thinking about it for a while," I said.

"You've been thinking about it for two years," he replied.

They gave me an alarm clock and a plastic garden gnome as a leaving present. Rudgie did my leaving speech. It was littered with jokes about cooking...

"A man goes into an Indian restaurant and looks at the menu. He calls the waiter over and says: 'What's a chicken tarka?' The waiter says: 'It's like a chicken tikka, but it's a little otter...'"

"Good luck with the cooking," said Sir Julian, squeezing my hand on the way out. "Enjoy the, um, truffles!"

I bought him some foie gras as a goodbye present, and told him to flame it in Armagnac.

"Oh no, I'll, um, eat it straight from the tin," he said, "perfectly pleasant!"

I packed my whites, cookbooks, and two knives and drove down to Cornwall. I had trouble finding the hotel. It wasn't quite the luxurious, five-star pad I'd been led to believe. It looked like a massive bungalow.

I met the head chef, Jez, at reception and he gave me a brief tour of the kitchen before we hit the bar. All the booze was free, and we downed pints and gin and tonics until about 2am. He then drove me at high-speed through the narrow lanes to his rented cottage. I don't know how he did it. I could barely stand, let alone focus.

The cottage had that damp Cornish smell that makes your skin feel clammy, but I was too drunk to care. Jez rolled up a joint, and even though I hadn't smoked since my student days, I joined in anyway, thinking it might scupper my job chances if I didn't.

After a few minutes, my brain had turned into a huge helicopter and I was fighting the urge to vomit. I kept concentrating on a brick above the fireplace, listening to his endless tales. The stories merged into one long boast, running seamlessly from one to another. The underlying theme was that I should be impressed by them all.

I can only remember snatches: the seven years he'd spent working under sushi masters in Japan; the time he'd got sacked as head chef of a top London hotel for wrapping his BMW company car round a lamp-post; the famous celebrities he'd cooked for; and the threesome he'd had with two 19-year-old models.

"The wife found out, but it was worth it," he leered.

He was bitter about the break-up with his wife, and how she was trying to "scalp" him.

"She wants £750,000 off me!" he moaned. "I told her I could buy a bullet for a grand! I meant it too!"

By the end of the night, his face had mutated into an ugly, jellified mass with two eyebrows and a nose sticking out. I began wondering whether the job was made up - whether it was a ruse to get the agency to send down fresh grockles. Perhaps they were in it together? I half expected Ian to walk out of a cupboard in a gimp mask.

Eventually I collapsed at 4am and was woken three hours later when Jez burst into my room shouting: "Morning chef!" He was already shaved, showered and dressed in his whites. His name was embroidered in fancy italics on his chest and both shoulders.

I staggered out of bed, put on my second-hand whites, and tried to sober up. The day passed in a haze. I was told to make a ratatouille, garnished with traffic-light colour sauces made from red, green and yellow peppers, in case any veggies turned up. Jez came over and tried the ratatouille. He told me to bung in a load of Worcester sauce and dried herbs "to give it some kick".

At one point, I almost staggered into a tall, smartly-dressed woman in the corridor. She was clearly the general manager or one of the owners.

"I don't think we've me before," she said.

I told her I'd been sent down by the agency for a cooking trial. She looked surprised.

"Oh, I didn't think it had got that far..."

In the evening, I worked on the garnish section. All I had to do was blanch mange-tout and broccoli and serve up ratatouille. It was very slow – there must have been ten customers in there. I looked round at the chefs – the last thing they needed was another pair of hands.

That night, Jez drove me back to his cottage. He rolled up another joint and put on a Garfield DVD. It was a bizarre experience watching a cartoon with a 39-year-old man. In the morning, he told me he would phone the agency and tell Ian what he thought. I drove back with absolutely no idea whether I'd got the job.

Ian phoned a couple of days later and said he couldn't get hold of the head chef. Eventually, he spoke to him and gave me the low-down. Jez said I'd fitted in well, was keen, but had a lot to learn. He said he was going to speak to the hotel directors about offering me a job. A couple of days later, Ian phoned back. It turned out there hadn't been a job there after all.

I WENT back to scanning the job sections, and then got a call about a gastropub in Cornwall that needed staff. According to the blurb on their website, they were looking for a commis chef or chef de partie "to help them in their hunt for their second AA rosette".

I could tell Ian thought I was just another romantic fool who'd left the rat race after watching too many programmes like River Cottage and Escape To The Country, and thought cooking and chewing turnips would be like living in an HE Bates novel, from the way he sold it to me. He kept mentioning they had their own organic vegetable garden, providing "ultra-fresh produce for the kitchen".

I had visions of Le Manoir aux Quat'Saisons, wandering over an oak bridge to pick leaf crops and herbs from cloche tunnels, and baby vegetables from the potager. But as I was to find out, rather than being an organic paradise, nurtured with seasoned compost and green manure, the "vegetable garden" was no more than a weed-filled gravel patch in a corner of the car park. They hadn't even bothered to clear the rubble away.

Ian emailed me the interview details, and I sold my car and bought a battered Triumph Dolomite for £500, and drove down to Mold, a tiny village that sloped down to a wide estuary. It had two pubs, a church, and a shop that, I would learn, only seemed to open for a couple of hours a week.

I parked in the square and walked up to The Crow. Only a brass licensee plaque differentiated it from the other cottages in the narrow high street. Through the blinds, I could see a plush, pine dining room with leather sofas surrounding a huge open fire.

I walked round the back and was met at the door by an elegant brunette in her late 40s.

"I've come to see June, the general manager," I said.

"Jane," she smiled. "That's me."

I looked at the piece of paper in my hand. The idiot had given me the wrong name. She told me to wait in the bar and went off to the kitchen to get Jules, the head chef.

She returned a minute later followed by a moon-faced man in his early 20s. He was much younger than I'd expected. He had narrow eyes and a sloping forehead, which stopped suddenly at the bridge of his upturned nose, giving him a look of perpetual surprise. He nodded, smiled, introduced himself, and then took me into the kitchen to meet the other chefs.

The starter section was run by Jules' 19-year-old hulking cousin Graham. John, the pastry chef, was a few years older and had a bad twitch. The first thing he asked me was which football team I supported. I said I didn't have a team, and he quickly lost interest.

Jules said there were two freelance chefs – Benoit and Greenie - who helped out most days. The other full-time cook was an 18-year-old Norwegian exchange student called Kolfinna, but she'd got the day off. She ran the garnish section, and had worked as a waitress in the restaurant before that.

I changed into my whites, and helped Jules with the fish as he studied my knife skills. There were none of the fish I'd learned to prep at Vieira. He got me to skin monkfish, prep gurnard and conger eel, and then fillet a 20lb salmon.

Miguel only bought one salmon a week, and poached it whole for the cold salmon mayonnaise salad. I'd filleted smaller round fish before like bass and mackerel, but never a monster that size. It was so big, only half of it fitted on my board. I don't know whether it was nerves, incompetence, or just the size of the fish, but I butchered it.

I found out later it was the same test Jules set for all the chefs he interviewed. At Rick Stein's Seafood Restaurant, the task

107

was to cook an egg. Apparently, Stein saw it as a good measure of a chef's cooking skills, but Jules chose filleting a massive salmon for some reason.

I also cocked-up the scallops. The pan wasn't hot enough when I put them in, and I turned them over using a pair of tongs which tore the meat. But I must have done something right because I got the job anyway. Either that, or they were desperate for staff.

Afterwards, Jane and Jules sat me down in a quiet corner of the pub and talked through the details. I was to get £12,000 a year plus tips. The hours were five split shifts a week, working from 9am to midnight.

I DIDN'T pack much stuff – just a TV, clothes, and some cookbooks. I suppose in the back of my mind I didn't know how long I'd stay. As I drove back to the West Country, I thought about turning round a number of times, and doing something else with my life. It had all become very serious. This was a full-blown cheffing job. I'd be working as hard as the Romanians, and would soon find out whether Mrs Henry had been right all along, and the glamour would wear off when I was working the same hours as her. I wondered whether I'd hear the ticker machine in my sleep.

It was a Saturday night and the village was like a ghost town. The air was crisp and smelled of wood smoke as I got out of the car. The chefs were in the middle of service, so I moved my stuff into a room above the pub. It was tiny and bare apart from a well-used bed and a crooked shelf.

I sat around for a while, staring at the walls, and then headed down to the other pub in the village. The Eel And Crown was a dingy, cold building with wood panelling and an outside toilet. The pub sign was of a badly-drawn eel staring out from a wreck. It summed the place up.

I found a table in the corner and supped pints of the local scrumpy. The thought of working the next day was doing nothing for my nerves. I just wanted to wake in a bleary state and discover it had all been a bad dream, and I was back at the paper, listening to Sir Julian's tales about Alan Davidson. I was on my fourth pint when the scrumpy kicked in. Snatched trinkets of conversation drifted over with the pipe smoke...

"Tries the patience of a saint that!" an old farmer said.

"Buggering hell!" a voice said somewhere.

"Had to go on a special diet because it's only a pup."

"I suppose that'll be something."

I found out later they kept the scrumpy in a huge barrel out the back and chucked rats in it. Once a cat had gone missing, and when they drained the barrel they found a collar with the name 'Tiddles' on it. It was all that was left. God knows what it did to your insides.

I left the pub well after closing time, clambered up the stairs to my dingy room, and fell asleep in my clothes. I remembered getting up at some point and looking for the toilet. The side door was still open and there was a gale blowing up the stairs. I passed someone in the passageway and muttered something.

An alarm was ringing somewhere in the room. I looked at my watch, tried to focus on the strange room around me, and then remembered the cheffing job. It was like I'd just poked a leopard with a stick and noticed the cage door was open.

I sprang out of bed and cleaned my teeth in the communal bathroom. It was a room about ten feet square, and served 15 people. The floor was covered in dirty aprons. I hadn't noticed the grime or smell before. The place was disgusting and I nearly retched.

I pulled on my whites, picked up my knife roll, and walked downstairs to meet the day. I was terrified, even behind the soothing, bleary state of my hangover. The chefs were moving about, turning on ovens, pulling food out of fridges and labelling contents. It was obvious I was a few minutes late. I couldn't see Jules, and only recognised Graham and John.

A chef called Greenie turned to me, and with a wide grin, said: "You must be Lennie. You're working with me today."

He got me working straight away, peeling and quartering potatoes for the Sunday roast. With a knife in my hand, a job to do, and no reason to attempt conversation, I immediately felt better. Greenie chatted away non-stop as I worked.

He told me he'd learned to cook in the Navy, had visited 58 countries, and planned to visit a whole lot more. It was his dream to scrape together £15,000, and move to New Zealand to open a small B&B on a vineyard. He told me tales about his days at sea, and the time he'd ruined 200 litres of white sauce, and was stabbed in the leg by a sous chef.

When the head chef walked past the changing rooms and found him strapping the wound, Greenie told him he'd forgotten he had a paring knife in his back pocket and had cut himself when he sat down. The head chef looked pleased with the answer even though he could see the pocket was on the wrong leg. His silence was rewarded. The sous chef became his "sea daddy" and protected him after that. Greenie was a good man – half-gypsy, tall and wiry, and as hard as nails – and we became good friends.

There were two others I hadn't met before: Benoit, who was acting sous chef and deputising as head chef in Jules' absence, and Jim the kitchen porter. It was Jim's first day too, which helped my nerves a little. He was a slow-witted biker, with cropped hair and thick glasses. He looked about 40 and for a

110

while I was pleased to have someone my own age there, but after a couple of hours I found out he was only 25.

Benoit was mousy-haired, bearded and angry. He'd finished a degree in ichthyology, and had gone back to cheffing to pay off a few debts while he looked for a job in marine conservation. He was most interested in hearing why I'd decided to ditch journalism to take up a low-paid job at the restaurant.

I finished the potatoes, covered them with duck fat, and put them in the oven, then moved on to the rest of the vegetables. They said Sunday lunch on garnish was the easiest job of the week, because the veg was plated up beforehand. I was soon falling behind though, and Benoit let me know all about it. Occasionally, Greenie jumped in and made a big dent on my pile.

I blanched cauliflower and broccoli florets, carrot batons, and green beans in a huge dipping pot on the flat-top, and then plunged them into iced water to refresh them. Then I arranged them on side plates and covered them in cling-film. For service, they were seasoned with pinches of salt and pepper, and clarified butter to make them shine, and pinged for a minute in the microwave.

Benoit came over at one point and shouted at me because the dipping pot was barely simmering. He pushed it back over the bull's eye in the centre of the flat-top, and the water began to bubble.

"It's got to be boiling," he barked. "Do you know why?"

I knew the answer, but I also knew it was better not to say. I'd been cooking for long enough to know that kitchens were all about getting on with the people you were crammed in with. Bollockings should be expected and accepted. And if you were a commis chef like me, you were the lowest of the low. It

111

didn't matter how old you were. Age wasn't respected, only rank. You had to unquestioningly follow the same military-based, robotic regime or you'd be thrown out on the street.

Benoit began a well-rehearsed speech...

"Vegetables lose their colour between 66C and 79C, which is why you put them straight into **BOILING** water to get them away from that temperature. You refresh them to stop the cooking by putting them in ice to get the temperature **DOWN** below 66C - so they don't go grey and manky, like those fucking beans you're just about to throw in the bin."

He strolled over to the pastry section, and came back with a handful of white powder and hurled it into the dipping pot.

"You can add a bit of bicarbonate of soda to the water as well – it helps keep the greenness...but I didn't tell you that..."

"Thanks, chef." I said, but he just glared at me and went back to his board.

We cleared down at 3.30pm, sharing the last few slices of beef and Yorkshire pudding between us. It was the only thing I'd eaten all day. When I asked Benoit what time I had to be back for evening service, he snapped: "That very much depends on how much prep you've got to do chef!"

I wandered back to my room for a snooze in the interval, thinking I'd keep an eye on the kitchen and go back when the others did. You could see the kitchen door from my bed, and they could probably see me too.

They started drifting in at around 5.30pm. They changed into their whites in the hallway, and I brushed past them to find Jules waiting for me at the foot of the stairs. He apologised for not being there at lunch, and said I'd be on the garnish section for the next two or three months until he moved me on to something else.

112

Running garnish meant being responsible for everything that went on the mains apart from the fish, meat and sauce. Every dish had a different permutation of baby carrots, baby fennel, green beans, mange tout, asparagus spears, cauliflower and broccoli florets. And I was expected to quickly memorise what went with what.

I had arrogantly assumed I might have the edge over them in the brains department. I'd even put "good memory" on my CV - but the whole thing was a nightmare. There were too many pointless quirks, like two asparagus spears for fish, while only one for duck or pork, so you didn't just have to remember the vegetables that went with each dish - but the number as well.

When an order came in, I'd count the relevant vegetables, and blanch them for exactly two minutes in the dipping pot. I made sure it boiled so fiercely, I had to keep asking Jim to flick the kettle on so I could top it up again.

Purees and other garnishes also fell into my domain. There was aubergine caviar for the bass, parsnip puree for the venison, sweet potato puree for the chicken, cassoulet for the pheasant and lamb dishes, fried polenta squares and caramelised swede for the duck, caramelised shallots and jenga-style chips for the fillet steak, and a whole host of other garnishes that seemed to change with the weather. There was no consistency to any of it. As soon as I nailed a dish, Jules changed it.

I got through the first day and had a few pints with Greenie, who was staying in the room next to me. Steve was behind the bar so we drank well past the bell, and then carried a few pints up to Greenie's room to watch a film.

The room soon stunk of grass. I don't know why I joined in. I knew it wasn't going to help me remember those plates. But I suppose with the age difference, I just wanted to fit in. And it turned out to be a good move.

"You know, when you first got here I thought you was a copper sent here to spy on us," Greenie said. He took another deep swig from a can, and hurled it into the bin at the bottom of his bed. "It weren't until I passed you that spliff I realised you wasn't."

He was streetwise alright, there was no doubting that. But from my days on the paper, I knew a lot of police officers who would have passed that test.

His conversation never halted, even through the film. But he was a good raconteur and full of stories. He told us about the other places he'd worked at in the West Country. The hotel in Truro, where he'd slept with four waitresses in his first week, and Larkham Castle, a strange place on the moors, filled with chefs who were too institutionalised to leave.

When I mentioned Jules and Benoit, he told me every kitchen had a whipping boy, and I just had to get good at the job so they picked on someone else. At Larkham, he said, it had been a chef called Fisty. I asked him why they called him that, and Greenie took a big drag, and passed it to me, giggling. Then he choked on the smoke and had a coughing fit.

"All the chefs got together in the kitchen, and told him they were all going out that day to get tattoos. They said they'd booked a load of appointments at the parlour, and Fisty had got the first one.

"So he goes down there, and they all follow him down an hour later to find he's got a viking tattooed on his arm...with fucking 'Iron Fist' written underneath. He says: 'What are you lot getting?' And they start laughing and say: 'Fuck off! It was just a wind-up!'"

I got out of there at 4am, and left them to it. I woke up four hours later. Every muscle ached. I got through lunch service, getting my arse kicked about by Jules, and then had a two-hour sleep in the afternoon before starting again at 5pm. I lay there in bed, the day already dark, reflecting on the new life I'd chosen.

I knew they weren't giving me the full treatment because I was new to the job. But it was hard being ordered about by people half my age. I had trouble working Jules out. There was no question he was highly ambitious and egotistical. But at times he seemed concerned, almost friendly. But then he would immediately launch back into his wind-ups and put-downs. The insults were getting worse too, as though he was testing my breaking point.

I was dreadfully slow and had a huge amount to learn, but some of the criticism was unfair. And if I ever tried to politely point that out, he would tell me not to answer back, and to just say: "Yes, chef." I was there to learn, but I was determined not to become a whipping boy like Fisty.

Jules was away that evening. He was doing a Desert Island Discs-style show for hospital radio. He was clearly anxious, and before he left, made me sit in his car and listen to the answers he was planning. He sounded like every other wannabe celebrity chef banging on about the importance of education, provenance, seasonality, and locally-sourced food. But I pretended to be impressed and gave him a few gentle pointers.

Then he made me listen to a recording of his hero Hugh Fearnley-Whittingstall on Radio 4's Desert Island Discs. He was reminiscing about his days at Eton, and how he developed an appetite for wild animals after strolling down to the Thames with a couple of half bricks stuffed into his overcoat, and nabbing himself a duck supper. He and his best friend roasted the bird with lashings of orange sauce.

He ended the show by saying the one thing he'd miss if he were marooned on an island would be chocolate. Jules said his would be foie gras – presumably from a brick-battered Thames duck.

Service was far more relaxed that evening with Greenie at the stove. We joked that Jules' groupies would have false teeth and hearing-aids. We tried tuning in the radio to laugh at his answers, but apparently the only place you could pick it up was at a garage a few miles down the road.

By the end of the evening, I was making fewer mistakes and had a grip on most of the garnishes. I had more drinks with Greenie that night, and watched another DVD. A pattern was developing. He drank far more than I did. He opened can after can, reaching into a 24-pack next to his bed. After he finished each one, he'd dunk it off his bedroom wall into a bin. Sometimes it went in.

Greenie spent the night lecturing me on how to get good at the job. He said the first trick in running a section was knowing where everything was in your fridge, so you're not flailing around during service.

"It's all about making the life of the head chef easier," he added. "That's how you get respect in a kitchen."

The next morning Greenie overslept, and the kitchen had to be opened up by Jules, who was furious to find he was the first one in. I put the morning's vegetable delivery in the dry-store, and then started on the spuds.

Kolfinna, a stocky, blonde girl with several piercings, was back from a long weekend. She had a bolshy attitude, and a habit of answering every order with an immediate: "No way!" And she was delighted when Jules told her she'd be moving off garnish to work on pastry with John.

She had only been there a month, and I thought that because of her age and inexperience, she'd be below me in the pecking order, but I was wrong.

"She could kick your arse on garnish any day – and she's a girl! And she's only 18!" Jules laughed at one point.

I don't know whether it was true, or some warped motivational tactic, but it worked and I immediately tried to step up my game.

There were two other new faces in the kitchen. A new commis chef - a well-spoken 18-year-old called Marcus - was to work with Graham on starters, and Jules was trying out a cook called Jack for the position of sous chef.

It turned out Greenie and Benoit were only filling in for Jules until he got a new team around him. Benoit was hoping to become a big fish in the marine world, and Greenie was off to the new fish restaurant being built at The Crow's sister pub, The Leg Of Mutton, a couple of miles up the road.

It had been bought by the property developer who owned our pub. Why he was opening a virtual replica just up the road was anyone's guess, but it seemed a guaranteed way of losing a lot of money quickly. The Crow was packed most days, but none of us were confident that would continue once The Leg – as it had already been nicknamed - opened. One of us would fall by the wayside.

Jack was a massive bloke from Birmingham, with a skinhead haircut and a scary face. He'd just come out of the Navy, and was obviously finding the transition to civvy street intensely frustrating.

The only person he seemed pleased to talk to was Greenie. They blabbed away in their secret Jack Speak, reminiscing about various ships they'd served on. They talked about babies' heads, eating irons, fresh hay, crabs, sun dodgers, and cheesy hammy eggy topsides. But the majority of their mysterious language seemed to consist of acronyms – SMPs, SOPs, UPOs, DCTs, the list seemed endless.

Jack was so wide, it was difficult to slide past him to get to the pass. And I didn't want to nudge him like a punch bag - he looked angry enough already. Jules worked quietly in the corner with Kolfinna, while Jack was put on sauce, which meant I was his bitch.

But I needn't have worried. When he was handed a copy of the menu, he looked at it, frowned, and said in his Brummie accent: "I don't understand a word of it. It might as well be written in fucking Spanish."

Graham caught my eye, and raised one of his huge eyebrows. Thankfully, Jack didn't cut the mustard, and Greenie was bitching about him in The Eel that night. Jules held his cards close to his chest to begin with, saying little more than Jack had enjoyed the day.

"I'm not surprised," laughed Greenie. "He did fuck-all! He just stood there with his thumb up his arse all night."

"And he butchered the salmon," I added slyly.

"It wasn't that bad," said Jules. "Well, better than yours anyway!"

"He'd only be here six months," said Greenie, changing tact. "He'd learn the job and then fuck off somewhere else and get a head chef's job."

Jules thought about that for a moment. Then he joined in, and we knew we were safe. None of us could imagine going for a beer with Jack, and that was the number one criterion for working in a kitchen. If you're going to spend most of your life with someone, you might as well get on with them. Kitchens are stressful enough, so there is no point in adding

118

bad chemistry to the mix. Problems are usually sorted out with fist fights in the chiller, and no-one fancied taking Jack on - not even Greenie.

I DID six shifts in a row, and was given two days off, but I still found it hard getting out of bed, even at 3pm. My bones felt shattered, and the arches of my feet ached from all the standing. Eventually I left my pit for the last two hours of sunlight.

I woke even later the next day, with vague recollections of ending up in some late-night diner. Someone had stolen some sauce bottles, and we drove through quaint Cornish villages spraying cars with brown sauce and salad cream. We put road cones on the roof and heard them come crashing down as we swerved.

The sun was streaming through the holes in my curtains. I looked out and saw the chefs scurrying around in the kitchen. It was a beautiful day, and I decided to get some sea air. I stopped at a village shop selling pasties, and struck up a conversation with an old Londoner. I asked him where there was a nice bit of sea to look at, and he told me all about Porbeagle Isle.

"It's about the best bit of coast round here," he said proudly.

I fell in love with the place immediately. It was a part-time island, with a sea tractor to ferry people across the beach at high tide, and rose out of the waves like a giant barrow. Half-way up was a pub, said to be haunted by the ghost of a smuggler. Perched next to it was an art deco hotel, built by an eccentric millionaire who'd bought the island during the Great Depression.

I watched the sun sink behind the huer's hut on top of the island, and then drove back to find Greenie holed up in his room, his foot in plaster. He'd been late for a train and

119

decided to take a short cut across the river. He was showing a couple of mates how to jump from boat to boat like a sea rat, when he missed his footing. He was drinking cans, out of his head on hospital-strength pain killers.

The first thing he did when he saw Jules was apologise profusely for having to take the next day off. Sick days are virtually unheard of in kitchens. I've heard tales of chefs who have soldiered on through service with their arm hanging off before calmly cleaning down and going to casualty. It's a macho thing.

Over the next few days, I slowly settled into the job. My first job of the day was to deal with the boxes of veg stacked up outside the kitchen each morning. I carried them over to the cold room, and then restocked my fridge. Then I would prep the vegetables, and make the risotto and purees.

Mash was the job I dreaded most. After the potatoes were cooked you had to rub them with the back of a ladle through a metal gauze plate to ensure there were no lumps. But you had to work quickly, and it was arm-numbing work. As soon as the potatoes began to cool, they turned gluey and grey and were impossible to force through.

The holes were so small, it took nearly an hour of rubbing to fill a four-litre tub. And I'd get through a couple of tubs a day, especially when the "mash monsters" were in as I jokingly called them. I tried to make a gag about them looking like the robots in the 1970s Smash adverts, but no-one laughed. Then I realised they hadn't even been born then.

I moaned about mash regularly – and even started having nightmares about it - until Greenie saved me. He waited for Jules to leave, and then hobbled over on his crutches and said it would be far quicker if I used one of the double-skinned sieves instead of the gauze, and forced it through with the back of a ladle. I tried it and the mash went through like butter. The result was the same too – the mash had the same creamy smoothness, it just took about a tenth of the time.

After that, I even began looking forward to making mash. But I always did it when Jules was out of the room. Head chefs favour the hardest method. It's pay-back time for all those years they got THEIR arses kicked around. There was only one good sieve in the kitchen and I guarded it closely, hiding it under my work station whenever I wasn't using it. Whenever anyone asked where it was, I just shrugged.

Any chef will tell you that prepping potatoes is the most time-consuming job on garnish, and you always do the longest jobs first. So after the mash, I cut the Jenga-style chips, so loved by gastropubs. The Crow's 50-seater restaurant was full most nights, and we were doing a roaring trade on bar food as well, so I got through about four 2ft-square boxes of maris pipers a day.

I'd cut the edges off each unpeeled potato to form a rectangular block, and then cut it into two, four, or six thick chips, depending on the size of the spud. The waste was horrendous, but Graham told me they only cost 3p each so I didn't have to be sparing. It was immoral filling the bin up with perfectly good chunks. Occasionally they were roasted or deep-fried for staff food, but mostly they just fed the rats up by the wheelie bins in the car park.

Once the chips were cut, I'd blanch them in the deep-fryer at 130C for ten minutes until they were pale and soft, and store them in plastic boxes in the walk-in chiller. When I had an order on, I'd fry them at 180C until they were golden brown. I'd put them in a bowl with towelling paper in the bottom to soak up the fat, season them with rock salt and cracked pepper, and then scorch my fingers as I arranged them in log piles of six on plates.

Next on my prep list would be cleaning the wild mushrooms that were foraged from the nearby moors. I'd pick out the maggots and forest debris, before trimming them and wiping them with a cloth. Chefs have different methods for cleaning mushrooms. Most don't use water, saying the "shrooms" soak up the liquid and the flavour is diluted, and they steam rather than fry in the pan.

When I moaned about my workload, everyone apart from Jules had sympathy. Graham, who'd spent a year on garnish at a Michelin-starred restaurant, said it was the hardest section because it involved the most amount of cooking.

"I reckon there's six times more than sauce, starters, or pastry," he said. "But it gets you fast at the job."

The whole time during service, I was running - boiling vegetables in the dipping pot, frying chips, refilling and stirring purees, cooking risotto, filling up the piping bag with more mash, and frying spinach and mushrooms.

As I got faster, I was expected to plate up the main meals as well. And then the bar orders would come in, and I'd fry battered cod, cook eggs for the burgers, and blanch pasta for the fish or chicken penne dishes. After a couple of weeks, I could tell I was getting quicker because Jules was bollocking me less, and had turned his guns on Marcus.

One night, I headed down to The Eel with Greenie for a late lock-in. We got back to find we'd been locked out. Jane still hadn't given us keys and had obviously assumed we were in our rooms. It was about 4am, and too late to call anyone, so we stood shivering on the doorstep for an hour. The car windows already had silver sheens of frost, and sunrise was still a couple of hours away. I was too drunk to think clearly, and had given up all hope, certain we'd be found frozen on the doorstep like grotesque, drunken statues in the morning.

At one point, I asked Greenie for feedback on how I was doing in the kitchen. I was surprised by the answer.

"Jules can't believe it," he said, "he thinks it's because you're older...he's comparing the rest of the commis to you – he thinks you'll go far!"

"Really?" I said, waiting for the wind-up, but it didn't come.

"Yeah, but don't forget my age," I said, blushing at the praise. "I've got an old body. I don't know how long it'll last..."

"Bollocks! You'll be alright. There's blokes in their 60s still cheffing."

I'd been scared to ask before. For the past two days, Jules had been winding me up by saying we'd got to have "a chat". My initial trial was up, and I was fearing the chop. Apart from a few late mornings, and days when I hated the job so much I wanted to walk out, I knew I'd been working hard and improving steadily. But one of the first things you learn in the kitchen is there are few compliments. The level of competition is intense, and the rivalry too precious.

Greenie began cursing again and hobbled up the hill on his crutches. He came back with a step ladder over one shoulder. I rushed to help him, but he was far more experienced at breaking and entering than I was. He soon had the ladder against the wall below my bedroom window. He forced the window and crawled in head-first, and for a moment his legs dangled unsteadily in the air before he disappeared. I followed, and even with two good legs it took me longer to get in.

Jules took the following day off and dropped by in the afternoon with a bag of spider crab claws he'd been given by one of our suppliers. He steamed them over salted water, and we sat there on the work surfaces, breaking the claws open and sucking the sweet meat out. Normally sitting was banned in the kitchen.

"Work surfaces are for rissoles - not arseholes!" Jules yelled at me the first time I did it.

The succulent crab meat reminded me of that scallop all those years ago, and for a while I sat there with a warm glow inside, feeling that I had at last found my purpose in life. While we ate, Greenie started a row about crabs being amphibians.

"No, they're NOT!" said Benoit. "They're crustaceans – they don't have a skeleton."

"Bollocks, they can breathe air and water so they must be..."

"No they're amphibious, but they're not amphibians – they have a carapace not an internal skeleton."

"What's that then?" said Greenie, pulling a see-through shard from one of the claws.

For a moment, Benoit was stuck for an answer, despite all his learning.

"That's not a SKELETON!" he snapped.

I WORKED seven shifts in a row and had virtually collapsed by the time of my next day off. I slept for most of the day, and then went to get a pasty and a cup of tea at a café in the next village. I never cooked anything in the communal kitchen because it was always in such a state. There were ketchup-smeared plates dotted around that had been there when I arrived. And it was where the dirty rags from the kitchen were stored and washed so it always smelled of sour food.

On my days off, I tried to get away from the pub - the whole place was suffocating. My travel to work was a single flight of steps, and I had to walk past the kitchen to get out, which meant I could never go anywhere unnoticed.

I sat in the café listening to a mad old woman cackling away behind me, and then headed off to Porbeagle Isle for some sea air. I walked along the darkening sands, the wintry wind whipping my ears, and mounds of seaweed piled up from high tide. There were neon ropes, plastic bottles, feathers, spades, and a pair of swimming trunks. If you looked closer there were dead crabs, mussels and limpets among the debris.

I followed the sands to the mouth of the estuary, where Atlantic salmon and sea trout swam to spawn. There were narrow caves with plastic lighters wedged into crevices, and granite steps leading up to the mansions overlooking the bay. They were blocked off by metal gates with no-nonsense signs. One said: "Private – don't be caught by tide. Guard dogs beyond!" I'd rather take my chances with rabid dogs than the sea, I thought, even without bacon in my pocket.

I hiked up to the ruined huer's hut on top of the island. It was just a shell with graffiti scratched into the brickwork. Someone had written "British built" and underneath someone had added: "So was the Titanic."

I thought about the fisherman who had sat there watching the sea all those years ago, raising the alarm when the waves turned silver. The boats would go out and surround the pilchards, and millions of fish were salted and packed into barrels. Most of them were exported to Italy, where they were used as anchovies. Then the fish stopped coming.

Half-way down was the Silver Sea Inn, a crooked building with stable-like doors. The tourist information sign said it dated from 1496 and was "said to be haunted by the ghost of an Elizabethan smuggler called Tom Trevisick, who was shot dead by customs men in a cave on the island."

I ordered a pint. I was the only one in there. The landlord, a strange, camp man with an acne-pitted face, was practising a Christmas carol, and tried it out on me. He'd changed the words to a story about a man dressing up in women's clothing. I warmed myself by the fire, wishing he'd go away. He stopped singing suddenly and pointed.

"Stare at the bricks to the right of the fire. Can you see it?"

"What?"

"Can you see Old Tom's face?"

I stared, as the landlord danced around behind me. Slowly I made out two dark patches for eyes and then a mouth. Then he pointed again.

"Look at the brickwork on the left! Can you see the face of the customs man chasing him?"

The grey stone formed into incomprehensible shapes, but this time no face. I tried again and shook my head.

"No, I've never seen it either," he laughed. "I think you've got to be pissed to see that!"

He came back with two more pints.

"But Old Tom, he's here alright! Sometimes I find myself talking to him when I'm on my own. I always know when he's here. He plays all sorts of tricks on me – I think he was quite a prankster in his day.

"When I first took over the pub, I was cleaning up and saw something out of the corner of my eye. I looked round and there was a lime in mid-air! It hadn't just fallen off the counter and on to the floor...it was about a foot above the counter. If the lime had just rolled off the bar, it would have gone down wouldn't it! It wouldn't have gone up!"

"I imagine so," I said.

He was beginning to unnerve me, and I still had to walk back on my own in the dark.

"I tell you, I saw it with my own eyes! I said: 'Tom, what are you doing to me?'"

"What did he say?"

The landlord looked slightly offended.

"Well he might have said something...in his own way. And then he started paying me more visits. I'm not afraid of him though, it's nice having someone around." He began to chuckle. "But Old Tom's a real nuisance sometimes. I hear him downstairs in the toilets, and I say: 'Tom, what the hell are you doing down there?'

"You know sometimes I go down there when I open up and the walls are all covered with wads of toilet paper! That's why I never bother to clean the bogs at the end of the night – you don't know what it's going to be like in the morning!"

I ordered another pint and drank deeply. I was desperate for the toilet.

"But it's useful when there's a stock-take," he added. "If there's anything missing, I say: 'Well, old Tom must have had that one!'"

I finished the pint and planned to get out of there immediately, when the door latch started rattling. I looked up, and then back at the landlord. His eyes widened like a cartoon mouse. The rattling got worse. A weight was pushing against the door. I could hear murmuring voices. It might have been Elizabethan.

"Never fails to amaze me," said the landlord, leaping up from his chair. He lifted the latch then hid behind the door. There was another push, and this time the door flew open, and two startled tourists fell into the pub.

"Arrrrrr!" growled the landlord, emerging behind them, with his fingers held up like claws.

The hikers darted back and then recovered their composure. The landlord was a complete lunatic, and I never went there again.

CHAPTER SEVEN

We hung the pheasants in pairs from nails in the dry store. We were told to keep the door shut so customers walking down the hill from the car park couldn't see them. But sometimes we forgot, and when they did see them, they were delighted.

They would stop and ask questions about how long they should hang for, where the pheasants were shot, and the best way to cook them. I was no expert, far from it, but it didn't stop me going into great detail.

Evidently, the world was full of foodies, who'd like nothing more than to give it all up and run a country restaurant. I wondered how quickly the lacquer would peel once they realised how much work was involved. But they were obviously passionate about cooking and fancied themselves in the kitchen.

Some would even try to press recipes on me, and I'd nod sagely before trumping them with another. Most were made up on the spot. I sometimes wonder whether there are manor houses in Cornwall serving pheasant a la quince.

The birds would arrive in the back of a Toyota pick-up truck. The poacher would tap on the kitchen window and bellow: "I's got another 50 pheasants for you!" In return, he and his mother and wife, who were probably the same person, would get a free meal in the restaurant.

We called him "Eyes Got" because he began each sentence with "I's got". Only Jules was pleased to see him. The rest of us cursed the pie-faced toad under our breath.

After they'd been hanging for a week in the dry store, we'd pluck them. Kolfinna was too squeamish, and would scream "no way!" whenever we asked her to help, and Jim was far too slow, so it was down to me and Marcus as the two other commis.

We would dress from head to toe in black bin liners, ripping the plastic for arm and leg holes. And then, like two forensic scientists who'd fallen into a bucket of tar, we'd begin the bloodshed. After 20 or so, the smell got sickening, and we had to keep the door shut throughout in case we were spotted by customers. It wouldn't have been the best appetite-booster to see us covered in guts, corn and feathers.

Plucking would have taken hours, so we skinned them instead. Jules would only roll up the breasts in ballotines, and confit the legs in duck fat, so it didn't matter whether we lost the skin. One of us would do the chopping, balancing a plastic board on our knees and hacking the carcasses with a machete, as we sat on two plastic boxes next to a growing pile of gore.

First the feet would go, and then the head. The chopper's "wing man" would then rip open the plumage on the neck, remove the cluster of yellow seeds in the craw, and then tear the skin from the breast, and pull the legs through. We would be left with a purple-blue carcass with red marks where the shot had gone in.

By then, the birds were plastered with feathers and entrails, and had to be washed carefully before the breasts and legs were removed. We sometimes used the carcasses to make game consommé, but generally they fed the rats.

Occasionally, we would get a bad pheasant, one that had been on its way out before it was shot, and the smell was horrendous. It was a dreadful job. But I became good friends with Marcus as we sat for hours in that dry store, sharing the gore.

To pass the time, he'd perform puppet shows with the heads, adopting a range of ridiculous voices. It's true what they say

130

about how working with meat or death gives you a dark sense of humour. The coroner's officers I knew from covering inquests had the blackest gallows humour I've ever come across. I suppose it was their way of coping with the job.

From time to time a waitress – or "Derek" as we called them - would come in to get butter or sugar, and squeal at the smell and the gore. That was when the puppet show would start again.

THE HOURS we were supposed to work were 9am to midnight. There was usually a split in the afternoon for two hours, but with the prep work piling up with the pre-Christmas rush, we were working right through most days.

These were known in the trade as AFDs (all fucking days) as in: "Are you busy, chef?"

"Fuck yeah, we've been doing AFDs all week!"

Our salaries were so low it meant our hourly rate was well below the then £5 an hour minimum wage. I was being paid £12,000 a year for a 14-plus hour day, meaning my hourly rate was £3.50 an hour. Tips were divvied up and came to about £100 a month, pushing my wage to about £3.90 an hour – still way below minimum wage.

When Greenie moved across to the fish restaurant, and did a series of AFDs, he worked out his hourly rate was £2.50 an hour, on a £16,000 salary. He was irritated by the agency chefs there, who often boasted about how they were getting £10 an hour. As a chef, it was always better to be on an hourly rate than a salary.

Once, when we had a surplus of pheasants, we took them up to The Leg and hurled them at an agency chef for plucking. He looked at them, and shrugged.

"That's alright, that's another £50 for me," he said. He genuinely thought he'd hit the big time.

ONE AFTERNOON in the split between lunch and evening service, we got some much-needed fresh air. Jules drove us up to an organic farm. He hurtled through the lanes, with the diesel engine screaming, 20 pheasants on the passenger seat, and the rest of us crammed in the back. A few minutes later, there were five chefs standing in the middle of a muddy field, each holding a knife. Only Jules knew why we were there.

The fields were drenched and inky green, and Eastern European workers were loading up crates of veg into trailers. We stood there in a huddle watching as the clouds darkened. A farmer in a wax jacket eventually trudged up from a neighbouring meadow, bringing the rain with him.

He was a miserable-looking man, and was chain-smoking black Superkings. We watched as a second tractor limped through the mud. More labourers were loading up boxes of black kale into its trailer.

They had doughy, rosy faces, and looked windswept and healthy. I looked round at Jules, Benoit, Graham and then Greenie. Greenie looked the greyest and most drawn, but we all had bags under our eyes, and fluorescent light-bleached skin.

The veg pickers worked fast, heaving and grabbing plastic crates and loading up the trailer, as their foreman yelled at them in Polish. It was something like "yedzia boat! yedzia boat!" Greenie said it meant "the boat is leaving". He'd learned it from a drinking song in Gdynia on the Baltic coast, but then he was full of stories.

The work was monotonous, but no more than chopping up box after box of spuds. They sliced vegetables and put them in a box, I opened boxes and sliced vegetables. At least they were out in the open air. Greenie must have read my thoughts...

"I couldn't work out here, it's too fucking cold," he said.

But I looked down over the meadow, holding my collar against the driving rain, and breathed deeply. The air was fresh-scented with compost and the mushy smell of goodness. The farmer gave us two boxes of kale as a sample, and then led us to the purple sprouting broccoli fields. He sliced off a bud against a wrinkled-walnut thumb, and ate it.

"Really crunchy," he said, spitting green and mauve spray at us. "And it's organic."

He said most of his veg was driven up to farmers' markets in and around London, but he wanted to sell it to local restaurants. He moaned about how he couldn't call it organic because he hadn't got Soil Association accreditation – even though he didn't use chemicals. He showed us a few buds that had disease, and told us how difficult it was growing without pesticides.

"It's all them pen-pushers in Brussels," he grumbled. "The bloody French wouldn't stand for it! They'd start burning bloody sheep or something!"

I'd only been in Cornwall for a couple of months, but I'd quickly learned to avoid the ranting farmers at The Eel, or the "Farmer Bin Ladens" and "Ooh Aar A" as we called them.

"That's alright, everything's organic on our menu," said Jules, winking at the farmer.

"Even the stuff that isn't," added Benoit. He was still smarting because we'd stopped buying diver-caught scallops.

The farmer lit a cigarette off the one he'd just finished, and handed us two empty crates. We tramped through the mud, hacking off buds. As more rain swept in over the hill and the sky rumbled, Graham started to moan.

"For fuck's sake!" he shouted. "What the hell are we doing out here, Jules?"

As Jules' cousin, he was the only one able to get away with any proper backchat. And the rest of us loved it when they argued.

"I've told you about that before," said Jules.

"What?"

"Stop whingeing!"

The sky was almost black, and then a blinding flash of lightning hit the ground near us. It was so loud, it took my hearing away for a few seconds. I looked down at where the lightning had hit, and thought about Sir Julian's tales, and whether it was a good spot for truffles.

Graham's hair was standing on end. He looked like he'd run out of a glue factory. We sprinted back to the car with the crates of veg, and he moaned the whole way back.

"What the hell was the point of that!"

"Of what?" said Jules.

"Of what! What do you mean OF WHAT?" His werewolf face was as purple as the broccoli sticking in my face. "Taking us to a fucking field!"

"Well...it's about prevalence...and that," Jules said, guppy-mouthed. "You know...about where food comes from."

"I know where food comes from! We grew up on a fucking farm, remember!"

"Well, you know...local-sourcing..."

In the mirror, his eyes were spinning like lottery balls.

"Respecting your ingredients..."

I'd seen him reading a 'farm to fork' article in a food magazine. I read it when he left it in the toilet. Provenance was obviously the new buzz word for chefs who couldn't spell the word and had no idea what it meant.

The others moaned the whole way back as we shivered in wet clothes. It was only Jules and me who'd enjoyed it. It was splendid getting out of the kitchen for some fresh air, but by the time we'd returned for evening service, the magic of those fields had long worn off.

All I could think about was how long it would take me to prep those four crates of veg. Jules wanted the kale and broccoli on that night's menu, and was already quizzing me about how many buds to put with the partridge, compared with the duck. And the parsnip crisps hadn't been done either...

STAFF MEALS were sporadic at the best of times, and there were days when we went without food. Nothing was bought in for us, and we had no time to go shopping ourselves. We had to make do with scraps from the kitchen, and food that was going off - the order was customers then stockpot then staff.

There was no rota for making meals, and only Benoit and Graham could be relied on to rustle something up, but they got fed up with carrying the rest of us. Whenever Kolfinna was asked she refused, saying she was too busy, even though she was always first in the queue when food was dished up. Marcus was the same, but he lived at home with his parents, and was well fed.

After a few weeks, the 'system' ground to a halt, and Jules banned staff meals altogether. Then there was a minor uprising. I told him it wasn't fair to expect us to work all day without eating, but he just rolled his fists next to his moon face and whimpered: "Boo-hoo! Boo-hoo!"

Benoit had the most effective approach. After coming back from a day off to find there were no meals, he said: "Alright, I'm going down the shop for a pasty – I'll be back in half-an-hour."

He came back seconds before service, and Jules reintroduced staff food that evening. He cooked the meal himself.

THE FREEZING temperatures in my room had left me with a nasty chest infection. The radiators had been on all night for the first few weeks, but then Jules went on a cost-cutting mission, and set the controls so the heating would go off at midnight and come on an hour after I got up. I had to sleep in three jumpers and a woolly hat, and even then the chill would bite through the duvet.

When I woke, the cold would be in my bones and I'd have a crick in my neck. I'd steel myself with a few swigs of vermouth, and put on my grease-spattered whites under the covers.

Once in the kitchen, the ovens would go on, and the air would hum with fat and sweat. The perpetual change in temperatures did nothing for my health. The clammy sensation of sweat turning cold on my back as I worked in the walk-in chiller was truly unpleasant. All the chefs, even those that didn't smoke, had hacking coughs, and before long I had one too.

But it was the bullying that was really getting me down, and I hated the way they treated Jim. When I talked to Greenie about it, he said it happens all the time in professional kitchens, and I'd just have to get used to it. It was the continuing circle of revenge. Cooks get bullied, then they get their own back on those below them.

136

Greenie said one chef he knew was working at a hotel in London, and was called in on his day off by an irate sous chef. He travelled from one side of the city to the other, on a succession of buses and tubes, and when he got into the kitchen was bollocked for not cling-filming a tupperware properly in his fridge. They made him recover it and sent him home. All that way for something that would have taken them a few seconds to put right. He left when they set fire to his pony-tail.

It wasn't nearly as bad at The Crow, but it was wrong of them to pick on Jim. Ironically, Jane's sister, who ran a bistro nearby, had sent him to our kitchen because she was worried he would get bullied anywhere else. But after a couple of months, the protection wore off, and the other chefs got irritated by his slowness.

Jules had given me a set of keys to the kitchen. He told me he was sick of seeing my veg supplies piled up outside the door every day where the rats could get them, and it was now my job to open up. That meant getting up half an hour earlier.

Jim was usually already there. He'd be standing at the top of the stairs, sucking on a cigarette, and in no hurry to get out of his biker gear. He only drove a moped but from the bright yellow leathers he wore you'd think it was a Ducati.

"Hello there!" he'd say each morning. He could never remember my name, but was always pleased to see me.

Jim lived with his sister a few miles up the road, and was probably the worst plongeur in the whole of Cornwall. It was hard to imagine anyone worse, but they still shouldn't have treated him the way they did. If you asked him to peel some spuds, you'd be lucky to get 40 by lunchtime. I never said anything - I always felt sorry for him. But sometimes Graham would pick up a potato and mock him, and challenge him to a race. Graham could peel a spud in under five seconds.

Jim's pace didn't quicken during the heat and stress of service either. He'd lumber past like a zombie with outstretched pans, chanting his favourite catchphrase: "Coming through! Mind your arses!"

"Coming OUT, mind your arses," someone would always shout.

Jim wore the same T-shirt every day. It had "It's not a bald patch – it's a solar sex panel" written on the back. I don't know if he knew what it said. He couldn't read or write, and we had to fill in his timesheets for him.

Every day, he'd ask what the time was, and someone would point at the kitchen wall and say: "There's a clock up there." He'd scrunch up his eyes and say: "Oh, yeah." Then he'd ask again a couple of hours later. At first I thought he had memory problems and had forgotten about the clock, then I realised he couldn't tell the time either.

The bullying seemed fairly mild to start with, nothing like I was getting anyway, but I felt sorry for him all the same, and guilty about not doing more to stop it. I still feel guilty about it now; sometimes I lie in bed in the small hours and think about it, and wish I'd made a stand.

It was Jim's job to make the tea, but he never remembered.

"Jim," Jules would begin. "Jim! Jim!"

Eventually he'd look round, blinking through steamed-up glasses.

"Hello there," he'd say, drying a plate in slow motion.

"Do you play golf, Jim?"

"I have done, yeah."

"You know when you start a game, what are those plastic things you use?"

Jim would think for a minute and dry half a plate. Then Graham would join in.

"You know! Those plastic things you stick in the ground at the start of each hole."

"Haven't got a clue. Do you know Graham?"

Benoit would then wander over and whisper something in his ear, and Jim would shout out "tee!" with delight. And then there'd be a chorus of "thanks very much Jim, I'll have two sugars!"

Other times, Graham would start it off.

"What rhymes with toffee, Jim?"

"Don't know..."

At some stage, a plastic yellow duck appeared in the kitchen. It squeaked when you squeezed it, which terrified Jim for some reason. They'd creep up behind him as he made soup in his sink, and squeak it in his ear.

When no-one was looking, he'd throw it in the bins at the top of the car park, but the duck always found its way back. Some days, they'd hang it from the hose by his sink, and he'd have to spend the day with its cartoon eyes boring into his bottle-end glasses.

One morning, Jim reached for the huge tub of Nescafe above his sink and screamed. I ran over, thinking he'd scolded himself on the kettle again. A yellow face was peering out of the coffee granules.

"That naughty duck," he squealed. "He gets everywhere!"

139

It returned a few days later, frozen in a bucket of water that Jim was asked to fetch from the freezer across the road. Its angry eyes looked up at him through the ice...

Graham switched the lights off and locked the door. He made terrible quacking noises, and threatened to throw him in the pond. Jim shrieked like a child. His sister had to come and get him. I'll never forget the noise he made. It was the sound of a pig in a barn fire.

JULES STARTED setting me time limits for jobs, and took a minute off each time I did them. Apparently it was a vital part of my training. He was just like the other head chefs I'd worked for. I don't where they come from, but there must be a gargoyle factory somewhere churning them out.

They are self-fulfilling caricatures. They bully and harass, and trample on those below them. When a head chef says something, you can hear echoes of all the chefs he's worked for. The same stock phrases are recycled from kitchen to kitchen.

"How long for that roasted veg?"

"One minute, chef."

"You've got 30 seconds."

How many times had I heard those words? Not nearly as many times as I'd hear them again. Charging around in a cramped furnace meant it was impossible to avoid collisions, and there was a constant call of "backs" as you worked. With the heat and bad tempers, it was suffocating.

"Sorry, chef," I'd say every time I knocked into Jules.

"You will be," came the stock response.

There was little originality. Chefs have their own language that takes all of a week to learn. The most common expression was "in the shit" – a predicament loved by co-chefs, who are only too happy to step in and help, so they can bring it up in the pub later. Each chef is painfully aware of his place on the totem pole, and any chance of promotion is grabbed with both hands, however hot the pan. Whenever it happened to me, Jules would say afterwards "you were in the shit there tonight" in earshot of my budding helpers.

Sometimes it just can't be helped, and customers will descend from nowhere. You'll be making risotto from scratch five times during service, while trying to cook an asparagus soup from fresh using ladles from the blanching pot for vegetable stock, and throwing in the red-hot bull's eye to get the broth simmering.

That's when the adrenaline kicks in – that's what professional cooking is all about, coping with anything that's thrown at you. You don't get the buzz every service, but when you're banging out plates, and the dishes look good, and you're not in the shit, in fact they're telling you to slow down because it's fucking up the chef on grill, then there's no sweeter taste.

Of course, the buzz doesn't last long – it may give you a warm, proud feeling as you down pints in the pub afterwards, it may even carry you to bed, sparking dreams of gastronomic greatness, but kitchen karma will ensure you get abused and kicked around soon enough. As Miguel said, you get good days and bad days in catering.

The only thing that made it worthwhile was a passion for the job. And I was beginning to doubt whether I had the required amount. Before I began my training, I'd chatter away enthusiastically whenever the subject of cooking came up. But as soon as I was surrounded by food, I wanted to discuss something else. Anything else. I stopped asking questions, and

141

wondering about techniques, and just got my head down and got on with the never-ending crates of veg.

I kept comparing myself to Jules and Benoit, questioning whether I had their passion, and knowing they'd been doing the job a lot longer. I certainly didn't have their manic energy. A good chef throws himself at any task – even mopping the floor.

"That's the poxiest cleaning I've ever seen in my life," Graham said to me once as I cleaned the flat-top.

He grabbed the half lemon I was using and scrubbed away like a gorilla on crack, and it was soon gleaming like a showroom Bentley. I'd never liked cleaning, and hated the fact it was such a large part of a chef's job.

I'd dream up chores in the dry store whenever they were deep-cleaning the kitchen. It was someone's job every few weeks to cover themselves in bin liners and climb up through the extractor unit to clean it. The thought of being asked terrified me. I'd been scared of enclosed spaces ever since I'd got locked in a campsite toilet as a toddler. But then I was probably too flabby to crawl through the ducting anyway.

Sometimes when I drained the deep fat fryer, or scrubbed the floor, I'd imagine Mrs Henry's big, ham-like face grimacing at me as I worked: "You want to learn technique – here's a mop! Learn that!"

When I first looked into professional cooking, all the chefs I talked to said I was mad for even considering the idea. "But then, you've to be mad to be a good chef," a few of them said.

But however insane my decision was, I felt alive. My emotions had become far more intense and colourful since I'd taken up the knives and bolted that hackneyed Fleet Street circus. There was always something to occupy you, and every day in the kitchen was somehow different. Not so much the work – the shenanigans among the staff.

One day, I phoned Colin at the paper to find out the gossip.

"Paul has taken a staff job, and Rudgie is moving on to online," he said.

"Is that it?" I asked.

There was nothing I missed about the humdrumness of their blanched lives. Sure, they were getting paid a lot more money than me, and had pensions and private healthcare, and could do things in their spare time, but there was no way I could go back. Not now I'd breathed life again, and gorged myself on the secret puddings. It'd be like turning the colour off on the telly.

But I still regretted the fact I rarely saw sunlight. My face and chins had turned a pallid, potato colour under the lights. Maybe it was all the spuds I was peeling? Maybe the starch was oozing into my pores?

There had been some beautiful sunny days, but the only time I saw them was when I walked from the kitchen to the dry store. I'd look up the hill to the oak tree at the end of the car park, and see it framed in golden light, its leaves blinking with amber. I'd pause for a minute and something would tug away in my chest, reminding me there was a lot more to life than food.

"It's a nice day out there," someone would say.

"Not that we'll see any of it."

And we'd look out of the window for a second and see the winter sun, and think of summer, and realise we wouldn't see any of that either.

During my splits, on the rare times I had them, I started walking around Porbeagle Island in the hope of getting some colour back into my cheeks. There was something peaceful and meditative in that stretch of coast.

It also meant I was getting fitter. When I started, I'd sleep through my splits, but now I was taking exercise. It had a lot to do with Greenie moving out – I was no longer staying up all night drinking and smoking.

WE WERE half-way through lunch service when Liz, the restaurant manager, came waddling into the kitchen like an asthmatic baby hippo. The only time I'd seen her move that quickly was to grab someone's chips. Something was definitely up.

"The AA inspector's in there!" she gasped.

"How do you know?" Jules' moon face had turned an unpleasant, porridge colour.

"I recognise him from last time," she puffed. "He comes in sometimes with his wife and kids...but he's on his own this time..."

"Jesus! What's he having?"

Liz stole a chip from a plate. "No idea."

"Well go and find out!"

She disappeared and returned with the rest of the Dereks a few minutes later.

"The boudin blanc and the lamb," they chimed. They were all enjoying the panic immensely.

Jules looked round the kitchen, and shouted at us to clean up. Inspectors sometimes ask for a tour of the kitchen, and he

144

was taking no chances. He ranted and raved, then yelled at me to make sure the veg was perfect.

All I had to do for the first course was pan-fry some spinach in clarified butter. Jules fried the boudin blanc, and let it cook through at the bottom of the grill. He rested it under the lights on the pass, then cut it into five slices on the diagonal. He put them in a circle around a small mound of spinach, then tried the spinach and looked slightly surprised.

"That's fine," he said.

He grabbed the pan of warmed, red onion marmalade I was about to use, and pushed me out the way. He formed the marmalade into a quenelle using two spoons, balanced it on the spinach, then spooned grain-mustard veloute sauce around the sausage with tear-shaped twirls. It was finished off with a sprig of chervil, like most of our dishes.

The dish went out and we got to work on the lamb. I can't remember if there were other orders at the time, but for 30 minutes there seemed to be only one customer in the whole restaurant. So much for everything Jules had said about customers being more important than awards. A few minutes later, Liz returned with an empty plate and said he'd enjoyed it.

I picked out three identical broccoli florets, and cut three carrot batons to exact length. I put a fresh pan of cassoulet beans on the flat-top, and heated them through. I was worried about the beans. They didn't have the same zip as the previous batch, and I'd secretly pepped them up with ketchup and Worcester sauce. I just hoped the inspector wouldn't notice.

Jules roasted the lamb and let it rest under the lights. I was about to plate up, when he pushed me out of the way again and snarled: "I'll do this!"

He nestled a mound of beans in the middle of the bowl and put a triangle of carrot batons around them. Where each baton joined, he placed a broccoli floret, and then put the lamb in the middle and poured jus over it.

After the meal, the inspector flashed an ID card, and summoned Jules into the dining room. He was gone for about 15 minutes. None of us knew if that was a good or a bad sign. Eventually, Jules came back in with his head down. None of us looked up. He walked over to my station and glowered. He looked ready to bite, and I scanned my station for hot pans. Then he lunged forward and hugged me. We had kept our Rosette.

"That wasn't at all stressful," he said.

"Really?"

"No, I was shitting myself!"

It was the first time he'd taken his armour off, and for a minute he looked like a pudgy schoolboy, who'd spent too much time in the tuck shop. His eyes were red and slightly watery.

"That was my first inspection," he said. "Well the first one as a head chef! The inspector said it was one Rosie, bordering on two. He asked about the boudin blanc, and I had to admit it was bought in. He said all the veg was perfectly cooked, but the lamb could have been a little pinker..."

I opened a can of Whoopass in my head, and fought the urge to dance around the kitchen, yelling: "In your face!" The veg was perfect, Jules' lamb wasn't.

"I was surprised, because we serve meat on the rare side, and sometimes get the lamb sent back. He said the cassoulet was nice and spicy, but the beans themselves lacked something."

146

They'd been soaked overnight, they weren't tinned. What the hell were you supposed to do? Grow them yourself? At least he hadn't noticed the ketchup.

"But he loved the chocolate marquise, and said it was easily two Rosette standard, if not three."

Kolfinna poked her nose in the air, as brazen as a dog at a fair. Jules kissed her and gave her the evening off. I spent the rest of the day on a high. My role had only been a cameo, but I was still part of the team that had successfully defended our cherished gong. And my veg was perfect! More than that, we were verging on two Rosies. Who said awards didn't matter?

WE DID an early Christmas lunch for the local CID branch, and that's when things came to a head with Graham. I was finding it harder than normal taking orders from a stroppy 19-year-old, and he would go berserk if I didn't follow his exact instructions.

He was the most naturally talented, and by far the fieriest, chef in the kitchen. And when I'd started at The Crow, Jules had warned me: "When he gets wound up, just ignore him. Don't say to him 'calm down' or anything, it just makes him worse..."

I'd given Graham a wide berth after that. I'd ignored his tantrums, and he'd swiftly made me his bitch. What irritated me most was his mumbling. And with my poor hearing, and the extraction unit going all day and night, I found it difficult to make out what he was saying. Sometimes I did it deliberately, but most of the time I just watched his lips move from across the room.

He would quickly raise his voice and get angry if he ever had to repeat an order. On his bad days, he'd moan about how he hated cheffing, and how he wanted to do something else with his life. But incongruously, he had more pride in our food than anyone else – even his star-gazing cousin.

Cathy, one of the waitresses, wandered in half-way through service. She said she'd been mauled by a couple of "drunken pigs", and her face was as sour as ever...

"Who sent out the terrines?"

She knew full well who sent out the terrines, but she always liked to stir things up.

"I did," said Graham, slowly. "Why, what's wrong?"

"Well, one of the customers would have preferred it if you'd taken the cling-film off..."

Her voice rose in pitch at the end of the sentence in a mocking fashion. There were a few seconds of silence.

"Fucking hell!" Graham shouted, suddenly exploding, and kicking a fridge door. "Can we have that with a bit more sarcasm next time! It's not as though this job's not hard enough..."

"Sorry, I'm just telling you," Cathy whined, grabbing a couple of plates on her way out.

Graham went into his usual tantrum about how he loathed cheffing. Then he exploded again five minutes later.

"The starters have gone on table four," he mumbled from across the room.

"Sorry?" I said.

"THE STARTERS HAVE GONE ON TABLE FOUR!" he yelled.

The change was far more irrational than usual, and a hot flash of anger rose up inside me. I was fed up with taking orders from teenagers. I rarely lost my temper, but I had a limit. I faced him from across the counter.

"Listen, Graham, we don't want to both lose our temper!"

He walked over slowly and stopped, his werewolf face a yard from mine. Just a chopping board and a knife separated us. His eyes took on a relaxed, dangerous look and he started nodding. He looked like he was trying to shape change into a wolf.

"Who's losing their temper? I'm not losing my temper!" he screamed.

"That's enough, both of you!" shouted Benoit from somewhere near us.

We both went back to work, and Graham made comments for the rest of service about the "repressive atmosphere" in the room. But the stand-off worked for a while, and it was a couple of days before he vented spleen at me again.

Afterwards, Benoit took me aside as we cleaned down, and gave me the usual chat about how commis chefs weren't supposed to answer back. He told me to bite my lip next time, and just say: "Yes, chef." But he knew how hard I was finding it working for Graham.

"I've had to face him down a couple of times," he confided. "But if he ever went toe-to-toe with me, it'd only happen once," he added menacingly.

A few days later, I went across the road to stock up on purees in the walk-in chiller, when the door shut behind me. The lights went out, a fan started whirring, and I was blasted with icy air. The panic hit straight away, and I thought I heard muffled laughter outside.

149

I don't know how long I was in there, but it was long enough to get mild frostbite in my fingers and toes. Eventually light trickled in and the door opened slightly. Graham had taken a few steps back and was watching me carefully.

"You think that's funny, do you?" I yelled at him.

Graham leapt forward and grabbed my whites and pushed me towards the chiller. I wasn't going back in there. I was terrified enough already.

I don't know where it came from – it wasn't a conscious decision – but my forehead slammed into his mouth. He looked shocked. His lip was split and his mouth filled with blood. He swung at me, but I ducked. I wanted to strike back but I could barely form a fist.

His next punch hit, and then the next, but the adrenaline was pumping and I couldn't feel a thing. Then he grabbed me, kneeing upwards towards my face, and tried to wrestle me to the floor. He was far stronger and heavier than me, and soon the muscles in my arms were flagging as he spat and snarled. Then the rest of them burst in and separated us. It took three of them to hold Graham down.

Jules returned the next day and told me to take a few days off until things had calmed down in the kitchen. He said it would be unpaid leave, but apparently that was my fault for "letting things get out of hand with Graham".

CHAPTER EIGHT

It was the first time I'd been back to London for three months. As soon as I stopped working, the tiredness set in and the chest infection that had been brewing turned into full-blown gammon flu (it started off as swine flu, but I was cured).

I lay in bed wheezing and coughing, and flicking through the latest cookery books. All the celebrity chefs had Christmas books out - 101 recipes for Brussels sprouts, and all that useful advice about how turkey leg meat takes longer to cook than breast meat.

A few days later, I got a text message from Jules saying the "air had been cleared with Graham" whatever that meant. I walked through the kitchen door, half expecting a punch from Graham, but he wasn't there. I glanced over to my station and spotted Marcus making mash - using my special sieve. He had a smarmy look about him too.

"I'm on veg now," he said.

It had all been decided in my absence. I was to move on to starters under the guidance of Benoit, and then after a couple of weeks take over the section myself. Graham was being moved to sauce, cooking the meat and fish for mains. I looked over to where Marcus was trimming beans, and told him not to forget the parsnip chips. I knew that section inside out.

Graham turned up the next morning, and we were shoved together and made to shake hands. Something had changed - he appeared less arrogant and confident than usual. He barely spoke for the rest of the day. Running the grill was new territory for him, and he was obviously nervous about messing things up.

151

That night, I gave Benoit a lift home, and we chatted about how I was finding it on starters. He looked at me and then smiled slightly.

"You know, now Graham's learning something new, he's in the same boat as you..."

I frowned, trying to read him.

"If you get fast at it...after all the things he's said to you..."

I still didn't understand.

"McJesus!" he said. "You can really BURN HIM! Churn out the starters! Force him to beg you to slow down – that's when you'll really know you've got him..."

"That's brilliant!" I said.

"He said the same thing to me when I started on sauce - he said: 'I'm gonna BURN you!' But there was no way he was going to get me on sauce! But, now it's your chance..."

I made it my mission to get as fast on larder as I could after that. Everything would still look good – I'd only take the short-cuts I could get away with – but the dishes would fly out as fast as the Dereks could carry them.

The first hurdle came, though, when the starters changed after the first week. Out went the boudin blanc (no doubt a throwback to the AA visit), the scallops with pea veloute and white truffle oil, the confit duck terrine, and the sun-dried tomato risotto.

In came tuna nicoise, scallops with vierge sauce, home-made gravlax with buckwheat blinis, smoked salmon salad, goat's cheese parcels with sweet chilli relish, game terrine, confit duck spring rolls, and a butternut squash soup with curry oil and a vegetable samosa garnish.

THE RESTAURANT was half empty in January as people tightened their belts after Christmas or changed allegiance to The Leg Of Mutton. To drum up trade, we started offering a two-course lunch menu for £12. The owner, worried about the new £5 credit crunch lunch at The Eel, had wanted to slash the price to £9.95 and include dishes like sausage and mash. But Jules convinced him we'd lose our precious Rosette if we went down that route.

There were three starters on the lunch menu, and they had to be reasonably cheap to make. They flitted between gravlax, confit chicken terrine, smoked salmon salad, confit duck risotto, goat's cheese parcels, and always a soup.

The soup varied between game consommé (made from the pheasant carcasses) with tagliatelle of yellow and orange carrot; mushroom soup with a morel-infused cappuccino foam; and cauliflower and smoked garlic soup with herb oil. For the bar menu, I made a tomato soup from red onions and tinned tomatoes. It was described as "roasted tomato soup", even though it had never been near an oven.

I'd make enough of each soup to fill two four-litre containers. I'd start by simmering a white mirepoix of onions, celery, garlic and leek whites for 30 minutes. Then I'd add three or four bay leaves, water, and the relevant soup ingredient - broccoli, mushroom, tomato, cauliflower, or butternut squash. I'd remove the pan from the heat as soon as the vegetables were cooked to preserve their colour and taste. Then I'd blitz the soup and sieve it. I'd always use Marcus' special mash sieve for that.

Benoit told me to season the soup at the end, gradually adding pinches of salt and black pepper until the flavour was just right. He lectured me about how adding salt in gradual stages has a peculiar effect on soup - it suddenly turns from an amalgam of competing flavours to a clear taste in just a few granules. He was forever bringing in cookbooks, and he

153

showed me a section from Herve This' book Molecular Gastronomy: Exploring the Science of Flavour. This did experiments with salt by giving people seasoned and unseasoned soups. Without the salt, they found it difficult identifying the type of soup it was.

The confit chicken terrine was probably the most 'cheffy' recipe on starters, and therefore the most time consuming. I'd rub 30 chicken legs with salt, pepper and crushed coriander seeds and leave them overnight to draw out the moisture. Then I'd wash and dry the legs, and cook them slowly for a few hours in duck fat until the meat fell away from the bone. I'd then carefully pick through the meat to remove skin, bone and gristle.

Next I'd overlap slices of Parma ham or blanched leek leaves on a sheet of clingfilm, and carefully lower it into the terrine mould so it covered the bottom and sides. Then I'd half fill the terrine with chicken, forcing it down to remove the air, before putting in a middle decorative layer of shredded ham hock or fried wild mushrooms.

I'd fill the rest of the terrine with chicken, wrap the clingfilm tight, put cut-out cardboard lids on top, and leave it under a 10-gallon oil can overnight. It compressed it so hard, the terrine never fell apart during service. For a la carte, I made a confit duck terrine interspersed with blanched green beans for colour.

The terrines were my favourite dish because they were the quickest to serve - and I knew that was the way to burn Graham. The better my terrines, the more people would order them, and the more I could make him sweat.

He'd fret if a table of six or more came in with more than two terrines. He knew all I had to do was cut a slice of terrine, smear the presentation side with olive oil to make it shine, and nestle it on top of a ball of dressed leaves.

Sometimes I'd put a quenelle of prune d'Agen chutney on top, other times a sprinkling of Maldon salt crystals. Of course, no plate was complete without the squeezy bottle, and I'd decorate it with a square of purple balsamic reduction, and an inner square of green herb oil. Sometimes I'd use a toothpick to zigzag the oils.

After a few weeks, I took over the starters section completely, and was a chef de partie in all but name and pay. I returned from two days off to find my fridge in chaos. The worst of it was the game terrine, made with chunks of marinated pheasant breast and venison. It was dry and hadn't been pressed properly because it kept falling apart when I sliced it during service. Half-way in, I discovered a bay leaf they hadn't bothered to take out, and that was the final straw.

"Christ who made this?" I said. "It's like trying to arrange a fucking jigsaw puzzle."

Jules came over and looked at the terrine.

"Are you blaming the two sous chefs?"

I saw Benoit and Graham move into the corner of my vision.

"I'm not blaming anyone, chef. All I'm saying is maybe the meat should have been cut up."

"You don't need to cut the meat up."

"Well something needs to be done. I can't be rearranging jigsaw puzzles every service."

"It hasn't been pressed properly," Jules muttered as he walked off.

I got to work on a new terrine that afternoon and the next day unveiled a perfectly-pressed example. The Parma ham looked like it had been wrapped at Harrods. Benoit was watching closely.

"Well try a bit then!" he said.

I carved him a generous slice. The mustard grain, chicken meat, and chopped herbs glistened in the morning sun. Benoit picked up the slice and threw it on my board like a spoilt child.

"Keeps falling apart chef! Wasn't pressed properly!"

He threw it again, but my terrine withstood his spiteful assaults. With ten gallons of crushing weight overnight, my terrines were bomb-proof.

I WORKED eight days in a row, and then on my next day off I went on a fishing trip with Benoit and Greenie. Benoit had somehow persuaded his mother to lend us her "old Hoseasons warhorse" for a trip down the river. The boat was about 30ft long and had three beds, a toilet, and a small galley kitchen.

I was leaning out of the boat when my hook snagged on something on the bottom and I tried to yank it free, angling the rod to one side. There was no give, and for five minutes I tested the strength of the line.

I got off the boat and walked a few yards down the riverbank, pulling the rod low over the river. Eventually there was a slight give. I kept pulling - something heavy was dragging along the bottom. I pulled again, reeling in some line, and the line stretched and looked like it was about to snap. Then something yellow broke the surface. I pulled again and a large plastic cage appeared and slipped back into the water.

"Quick!" I shouted to the others. "Have a look at this."

Greenie and Benoit looked over from their rods, and made wanker signs. We hadn't caught anything all day.

"LOOK AT THIS!"

Greenie eventually wandered over. He grabbed the line, and pulled out a barrel-shaped trap. There must have been 30 fat crayfish in a wriggling mass. There was a sticker on the side saying "Property of the Environment Agency".

"Get a fucking pot!" he shouted.

He poured the crayfish into the saucepan, and pushed the lid down to stop them escaping. One or two hit the side of the pan, and quickly made a dash for freedom. Somehow they knew where the river was.

I went to grab them but they lashed at me with their claws, sitting back on their tails like miniature gladiators, with their pincers held aloft. Greenie poured out the last of the crayfish, and a gnawed fish head fell on to the river bank.

"Put the bait back in, or they'll know we've been here," hissed Benoit.

He was looking up and down the river anxiously. He said they were the American signal crayfish that had wiped out the UK's native species, so we were doing our bit for ecology, but he knew that getting caught poaching crayfish wouldn't help his chances of getting a job as an ichthyologist.

A length of thick string was tied to the trap. I followed it along the river, and 20 yards later another trap emerged from the mud. There must have been another 50 crayfish in there. We could hardly get the saucepan lid on.

Benoit started the boat engine, and we headed back up stream. I boiled a kettle on the spluttering galley stove and examined our catch. The pan had a glass lid and their beady

157

eyes peered at me suspiciously. Ten minutes later the kettle started to whistle. It was a sound the crayfish hadn't heard before, but somehow they knew something was wrong, and began rattling the lid. Then we realised we didn't have any salt.

Greenie said we'd ask for some at the next lock, but Benoit was worried it would draw too much attention. A request for salt could mean only one thing – a bucket full of poached crayfish. The gas was so weak, I could only boil a few at a time. After two batches the water had turned into a thick yellow soup.

I drew the curtains as we went through the lock. Greenie jumped out to deal with the ropes and keep the lock-keeper chatting. The sweet, forbidden smell of boiled crayfish wafted out into the cold air. I carried on my scurrilous work as he chatted away about red boards, and currents, and how high the weir was, and how to catch eels with a ball of wool. We had gone through another lock, with the same elicit bouquet pouring out, by the time I was on my last batch.

We moored up and got to work. The crayfish were a beautiful rusty vermillion. We cracked them open with our hands and picked out the black intestinal sac that ran down their backs. I sucked out the meat from a head, the same way I do when I'm peeling prawns. It was a bad mistake. Yellow and green river gunge shot in my mouth. It was as bitter as wormwood, and took a pint of water and a few swigs from the gin bottle to banish the taste.

Soon there was a funeral pyre a foot high of shells and claws. I'd been thinking of a recipe for the past hour – I'd solve the salt problem by frying them up with bacon rashers. Being freshwater, and especially if the head meat was anything to go by, they'd need as much salt as possible.

I fried chopped bacon in two scoops of salted butter, and threw in a few ripped sage leaves I'd stolen from a lock-keeper's garden. Then a squeeze from the lemon we'd been saving for our vodka-tonics. The juice fizzed in the pan. I threw in the tails - and a buttery, bisque-like aroma filled the galley.

I poured the crayfish and butter sauce on to three plates with thick doorsteps of bread for the mopping. We sat there in silence, making occasional gluttonous noises, while the rain beat hard against the boat.

Our plates were soon spotless with the bread-wiping, and we sat there with our bellies strangely full, reflecting on what we'd just done, and what a delicious supper we'd had, and how much peeling goes into making just one Prêt A Manger sandwich. I know boats and fresh air make you hungry, but I can honestly say it was one of the best meals I've ever had.

MY FIRST job of the day on starters was washing and picking three tonnes of lettuce - about enough to fill 23 Volvo estates. There were four types of leaves – rosso, oak leaf, frisee, and radicchio. I'd pick each leaf off, carefully rip it into strips, and throw away the spine.

The lettuce had to be washed three times until the water was clear, then dried in a salad spinner. It was a dreadful job in winter – the water was so cold that after an hour my hands would go completely numb and I'd lose all sensation in my fingers, and if you ever got caught skimping on the washing, there'd be trouble.

Once my tubs were filled with endless prepped leaves, I'd move on to the terrines, soups, and whatever else needed doing. I'd prep the garnishes – chopping chives and parsley, picking chervil sprigs, browning pine nuts, making tomato concasse, and blanching green beans for the tuna nicoise salad.

My set-up for service was a bottle of olive oil and roe dust for frying scallops, various reductions in the reach-in fridge, salt, pepper, mushroom dust, various chopped herbs, salad dressing, and two tubs of leaves. I also had a spoon pot, and the only two saucepans that worked on the induction hob hidden in my drawer.

The scallops that arrived every morning varied in quality. Sometimes they were small and grey, and looked like they'd been on the boat for a few days. Other times they were beautifully sweet and pearl white. After two bad batches in a row, we started buying them in the shell and shucking them ourselves. Sometimes they were so fresh they sprang back as you prodded them.

Benoit, of course, knew all about scallops and how the boats that fished them wrecked the seabed. He grimaced as he showed us the shells, and the chips round the edges caused by dredging. He said that was how you could tell if they were dredged. We were still describing ours as diver-caught.

One day, I put a copy of the menu in front of him just to watch his reaction. He immediately became incensed and yelled at Liz to change it.

"If these are diver-caught," he said, holding up the battered shells like a court exhibit, "then I'm a monkey's fucking uncle!"

We served the scallops with a vierge sauce as both a starter and a main. I'd dry roast coriander seeds in a pan and crush them with the end of a rolling pin, releasing a wonderful, nutty aroma. I'd add olive oil, white wine vinegar, very finely diced red onion, tomato concasse, and chopped garlic, parsley and chives.

The vibrant pink and green sauce looked wonderful with the golden-brown scallops. I'd coat them in scallop dust and fry

160

them in a sizzling hot pan on my induction hob for 30 seconds on each side, so they were caramelised on the outside and marshmallow-soft in the middle. I liked to use the hob because it meant I didn't have to fight for stove space on the other side of the kitchen, and there was no residual heat so I could put lettuce nearby without it wilting.

After a couple of weeks, I started tinkering with the vierge sauce recipe, and added a few crushed fennel seeds. Underbelly of aniseed, and thoughts of France, I mused. In fact, I was so proud of the addition, that in a moment of madness I told Jules.

"Who told you to change it?" he snapped.

I bit my lip and made a new batch of sauce without the fennel. He was just like all those other automatons that come out of Michelin-starred restaurants.

After a few more weeks, I'd got to grips with the menu, but I was still having problems with the slow-roasted, spiced pork belly with apple wontons. It wasn't the pork belly - it was the wontons.

I'd put a spoonful of spicy apple puree in the middle of a wonton skin, and twist the sides to form a tortellini shape. After a few hundred, and some atrocious early efforts, I'd got the hang of them. But the trouble was storing them. They'd go slimy in the fridge, and when I picked them out would stretch like yellow chewing gum.

I tried putting holes in the clingfilm to give them air, but it made no difference. I took the clingfilm off altogether, but it was still no good. In the end, I thought I'd cracked it by laying them in semolina flour. But even then they would go soft after a few hours, and I'd have to make a new batch before service.

I hated the wontons, but the worst job of all was the balsamic reduction. I had no idea why we didn't just buy it in. I'd boil

161

down gallons of balsamic vinegar until it was thick syrup, and had filled the kitchen with noxious fumes that got into our lungs and made our eyes smart. After an hour of boiling, it felt like my chest was being eaten away. It took litres of vinegar just to fill a squeezy bottle, and with the rate I was going on the terrines, I was getting through bottles of the stuff a week.

I made ten portions of each starter for service, and 20 of the goat's cheese parcels because they were easily the most popular dish, and the most profitable. They scarcely cost 50p to make and sold for a fiver.

I'd cut a slice from a goat's cheese log and egg wash a spring roll wrapper. I'd lay a circle of spinach leaves in the centre of the wrapper, put the cheese on top, fold the left side of the wrapper into the middle, and then the right side over, and finally the top and bottom sides into the centre to make a square parcel. I'd have to egg wash each fold well and pull it tight, or they'd explode in the fryer.

The parcels were served on salad leaves with sweet chilli relish. Graham had given me the recipe for the relish. He was very proud of it. It had been entrusted to him like a dusty heirloom by his old head chef, and he claimed "it couldn't be beaten".

It was incredibly simple to make – you just fried chopped tomatoes and sliced red chillis in sugar, vinegar and spices, and then reduced it to make a jam. It tasted alright, but the twigs of coiled tomato skin looked terrible.

I pointed it out to Jules one day, and he told me to skin the tomatoes. When I reminded him that it was Graham's precious recipe, he just said: "Well, I don't think he's thought it through."

I started tinkering with the recipe further, and then Graham spotted the revamped relish on a particularly busy night.

"Why the hell has the chilli relish been changed?" he yelled. "That recipe was perfect. It was tried and tested!"

A row started and Jules tried to defuse it.

"Why the fuck did you tell Lennie to change it?"

"I only told him to skin the tomatoes!" Jules whined.

"Why the fuck did you tell him to skin the tomatoes?" screamed Graham.

"Well...because you don't want skin in it..."

"It's RUSTIC, for fuck's sake!"

Jules realised the only way out was to soothe his cousin's monstrous ego. He dunked a fat finger into the relish, and grimaced like a baboon pissing glass.

"I didn't tell him to make it like that!"

We all looked at the neat squares of tomato in my relish. The bile instantly rose inside me. I don't know why it got to me so much, but I wasn't having them slag off my chilli relish. I was making the stuff before Graham was even a twinkle in his uncle's eye.

But it wasn't just dented pride. It was because I'd taken so many bollockings over the months for mistakes I'd made, I wasn't going to take them when I hadn't. Also, there was no longer such a yawning gulf in our cooking skills, and I was beginning to notice flaws in their knowledge.

Liz walked in with some dirty plates.

"They LOVED the goat's cheese parcels!"

She scraped the empty plates and handed them to Jim.

"Oh, and they asked if they could have the recipe for the chilli sauce, Lennie."

"You better ask Graham for that," I said bitterly.

ONE DAY I heard those golden words I'd waited so long to savour. Four tables ordered at the same time, and I'd got those out, and was dealing with a fifth when I scuttled past Graham to the fryer.

He was frantically plating up five sea bass, while flashing steaks under the grill. He spotted the six goat's cheese parcels on my tray, and alarm spread over his lupine face. He attempted a smile. Then he whispered those wonderful words. I can still hear them now. They brushed my ears like heavenly mist.

"Can you slow those up a bit, or I'll really be in the shit..." he mumbled.

I pretended not to hear. The words were too pleasing, too magnificent.

"What?" I said.

"Can you slow those up a bit, or I'll really be in the shit..."

I stared at him for a second, remembering all the insults and strops. And then I went back to my board and pretended to be busy for a few minutes. The Dereks were soon hanging about, nibbling my garnishes like rabbits, so I walked back over to the fryer and chucked in the parcels. Graham nodded at me on the way back. It was the same feeling I'd had when I'd been called "chef" at Rick Stein's, but much, much better.

JULES SOMEHOW found himself a girlfriend. He started taking weekends off, and came in full of tales of his sexual exploits.

"Posh girls are so dirty," he kept boasting.

One weekend, his girlfriend decided to delay her return to Bristol, and he took the Monday night off as well. A table of three came in and ordered three starters, and three starters as mains. It messed everything up on my station as I grappled with the other tables. I sent out their starters, and then got to work on their wild mushroom risotto, pork belly, and scallop salad. I double-checked with Cathy, and they did just want their mains starter-size.

Cathy, who had just been promoted to assistant restaurant manager, held up the pork dish and examined it closely under the lights, and then did the same with the scallops.

"Don't we usually serve the scallops in a circle round the salad, not a square?"

"That's for the scallops with vierge sauce," I said. "The salad's in a square!"

She looked in no hurry to move, and prodded one of the scallops.

"Are you sure?"

There was something in Cathy's nature that just stuck in your gut. It wasn't just the way she openly stole food from plates, it was the sarcasm. I was doing the job well enough, and no longer saw myself as a commis, and I wasn't going to take advice on plating up from a biscuit-muncher.

"Just fucking TAKE them will you!" I shouted.

Her reaction was immediate and explosive. She clearly saw me as nothing more than a jumped-up commis.

"Don't fucking tell me what to do you fucking prick!"

Her freckled face turned a horrible bright purple. Benoit, who was doing pastry that night, quickly stepped in.

"Look, don't just stand there with the plates in your hand, put them back under the lights if you're not going to take them!"

"I'm not going to take that from him!" Cathy shouted back.

"CUSTOMERS ARE WAITING!" yelled Benoit.

Liz waddled in and the plates disappeared. Cathy was sullen for the rest of service, no doubt planning her attack. Then another fight broke out. Liz asked Benoit why there wasn't any chocolate sauce on one of the desserts, and he yelled at her to "get the fucking plates out!"

I was clearing down with Marcus when one of the desserts came back. Cathy looked delighted as she broke the news.

"They said the apples in the crumble were too sour..."

They had hardly touched the dish. We all tried it. It was as sour as week-old yak's milk in the Danakil sun. Even the ice cream couldn't save it.

"Kolfinna hasn't cooked down the apples enough!" said Benoit.

It would have been churlish to mention that she'd forgotten the sugar as well. We sent out a free dessert, and were standing out the back sharing a smoke, when Liz and Cathy came out.

"Do you want the bad news or the bad news?" said Liz. "The table that sent the crumble back were AA inspectors!"

"Bollocks! There were three of them!" said Benoit.

"Well the woman said they don't usually go out together..."

"She showed us her card and everything!" added Cathy.

Depression hit us like a giant anvil.

166

"She asked whether the head chef was here and we said it was his night off. So she said she would speak to him another day..."

I drove Benoit home and we went through the dishes they'd had. Six of the nine had been mine.

"Did you put parmesan in the risotto?" he began.

"I even put mushroom powder in to pep it up a bit."

"What about the pork belly..."

But we both knew the damage had been done. To not like a dish was one thing, to send it back was another. Benoit decided to phone Jules – even if it was his night off. I caught the occasional word. It was a short conversation.

"Jules was pretty philosophical about it," Benoit lied afterwards. "He was good enough to say the same mistake would have happened if he'd been there."

We all knew the apple filling should have been tasted before it went out. I stayed at Benoit's house that night. In the morning, I suddenly remembered that with all the drama, I'd forgotten to write out a prep sheet for the next day, and hadn't checked through my fridge. To make matters worse, I had two days off, and Jules was covering my station.

When I went back in, no-one would look me in the eye. I thought it best not to ask about the AA inspection. Jules came in and flew into a rage. I'd never seen him like that before. Normally when he was in a bad mood, he just went quiet. He started pulling tupperwares out of my fridge and throwing them against the wall.

"You really left me in the shit – and I mean that! You really stitched me up," he yelled. "Look at those fucking wontons! I couldn't use any of them. And there's no dates on anything!"

167

He then walked over and snarled, as if reading my mind: "And that apple crumble - that was all of our fault!"

"Yes, chef," I said.

I was furious but I kept quiet. I knew what I had to do. I hadn't made a dessert in the seven months I'd been there. I packed my bags that night and drove back to London.

A few days later, I got a call from Greenie. It turned out those two evil waitresses had made the whole thing up.

CHAPTER NINE

I stared at the email, wondering whether it was a cruel joke from one of those mean bastards at the paper. I'd applied for jobs and stagier placements (a cheffing term for unpaid work experience - or modern day slavery) at some of Britain's top restaurants and I'd pretty much forgotten all about them.

It was from the human resources manager at the Fat Duck, a three-star Michelin restaurant famous for concoctions like snail porridge, bacon-and-egg ice cream, and a food poisoning outbreak that struck down 500 diners.

"Further to our recent communications, please find attached confirmation of your stage placement here," it began.

I couldn't believe it. I was going to learn how to cook with liquid nitrogen, ice baths, dehydrators, vacuum pumps, and all manner of weird science in the gastro-wizard's lair. Secrets from the great culinary alchemist Heston Blumenthal himself. Crumbs from the table of the Mad Hatter's tea party. I was so excited I almost wept. It felt like I'd opened a chocolate bar and found a golden ticket for a tour of Willy Wonka's chocolate factory.

Of course, the work was unpaid. And there was a rather disconcerting mention that my "actual" hours of work would be shown on the departmental rota when I got there. But how many people could say they'd cooked in a restaurant that had recently been voted by a panel of 500 chefs and industry experts as the second best in the world? It would be something to tell the grandchildren if I ever had any – even if it was only as a galley slave.

I looked at the menu - sardine on toast sorbet, salmon poached with liquorice, hot and iced tea, chocolate wine et al. The man was clearly insane, and that's what I liked about him.

That and him being an entirely self-taught chef, who'd only managed a week in a professional kitchen before opening his own restaurant.

There were three forms I needed to download and sign, including a "food handler's declaration" ordering staff to report immediately to the manager if they developed any illness involving vomiting, diarrhoea, septic skin lesions, ear or eye discharges, or any other unpleasant condition. At the bottom, it warned that "knowingly giving false information may result in disciplinary action".

A couple of days later, I got another email. This time it was for an interview for the position of commis chef at Gordon Ramsay's flagship Royal Hospital Road restaurant in London. The prospect of working there was even more frightening than the Fat Duck, but then the work was paid – not that I was likely to get the job.

I phoned Benoit and asked him for advice. He said Ramsay's kitchens were infamous for being the toughest in London. But if I could last there, I'd be able to do anything.

"If you hand in a CV with 'two years at Gordon Ramsay's' on it, it'll tell even the most hairy-arsed chef everything they need to know," Benoit added. "But I should think about it first – it'll be fucking hard work!"

He said the Fat Duck had a reputation for being more relaxed and a lot less aggressive than most Michelin-starred restaurants. Regardless though, he said, I should go along for the interview and decide from there.

I went along to Ramsay's headquarters near Victoria, and was given some forms to sign while I waited for the human resources manager. They took a photocopy of my passport, and eventually the HR woman arrived. She was short and tough-looking, and immediately made me feel ill at ease. Perhaps you had to be to work for the famously volatile chef?

"You know the chefs work 18 hours a day here?" she said almost immediately.

I shrugged and pretended to let the news flush over me. I said I'd done a few 18-hour days in Cornwall.

"Well, it's 18 hours EVERY day here," she said, studying my reaction.

She told me to think about it and said they were looking for staff at the Boxwood Café in Belgravia as well as Royal Hospital Road. I wasn't in the least bit surprised. Then she phoned the kitchen and said I could do a trial on the Saturday. I shook her hand and walked out. We hadn't even talked about money.

By the time I'd reached the front door, I'd made my decision. Even at 19, the hours would have killed me. I'd have to start work at 8am and finish at 2am. In the six hours between shifts, I'd have to get a night bus home, sleep, wash, feed myself, and then get back into work. I'd probably be lucky to get three hours sleep before I had to do it all again.

I knew I wouldn't even last a day so I emailed Ramsay's office and cancelled the trial. Then I called the Fat Duck and was told I could start my stage in two weeks. I just hoped it wouldn't be the same ludicrous hours.

I ARRIVED there at 8am on a Monday morning after a fitful night's sleep worrying about how the hell I'd cope with working in the second best restaurant in the world.

The Fat Duck was perched on a blind bend in the centre of Bray, a celebrity-filled, middle England haven of ostentation, and was far smaller than I had imagined. It had a tiled roof, flesh-coloured walls and gunmetal grey windows, and could

171

have been any one of the thousands of trendy gastropubs that had spawned across Britain.

But the pub sign, with its webbed and feathered knife and fork design, spelled out everything you needed to know about the quality of the food within. This was the Mecca of British gastronomy, the place Gordon Ramsay and Marco Pierre White used to go on their days off, the kitchen of a man described by The Guardian as the "most talented chef this country has produced for a country mile". I stood outside the front door, and spotted Blumenthal's name on the brass licensee plate. I could almost smell the nitrogen.

A waiter ushered me through a plush, lime and yellow dining room to a tiny kitchen at the back. A chef with a large, squashed face and prominent teeth was leaning in the doorway. He looked at me nervously, and then became relaxed and surly when I told him I was on a stage as well.

"Oh, I thought you were one of the chefs," he said.

I was directed out to the garden, past the nitrogen gas canisters, to a row of sheds that made up the stores, and was told to change in Shed Eight. It was no bigger than anything you'd find on an allotment, and served the 20 or so chefs who worked in the main restaurant. It quickly became clear that the three-star luxury extended no further than the dining room, and space in the 16th century former inn was as tight as a camel's arse in a sandstorm.

I changed into my whites, and tried to hide the plastic Tesco bag that carried my only two knives under my arm. There were two other stagiers waiting outside the kitchen by the time I got back. They had professional knife bags, no doubt containing a frightening array of razor-sharp blades.

As well as Paul, the nasally chef with the buck teeth, there was a wiry young Swedish chef called Andreas, and a hairy

Spaniard in his 20s called Jesus. Jesus was on a two-day trial for commis chef, and had spent the past month doing a tough stage at Michel Roux Jnr's Le Gavroche in London.

As we stood around by the tills at the front of the pass, chefs of all nationalities walked past and introduced themselves.

"Are we pleased to see you guys!" said a portly, red-faced American cook called Danny. "We've been running low on stagiers lately!"

What had they been doing with them? I just hoped they weren't experimenting with Demon Barber sorbet up in the lab. Then a wild-eyed Scot with a smile like a shipwreck raced out of the kitchen with a tray of mango jellies. He introduced himself as Jocky, and said he was the head pastry chef.

"Boys, we're doing a function for 80 at Le Gavroche," he bellowed, "got to wrap all these..."

He said they were working on edible wrappers in the lab, but hadn't cracked them yet. He showed us how to wrap each sweet, twisting the ends in opposite directions, and then vanished back into the broom cupboard kitchen.

We stood in a line carefully twisting each sweet like our lives depended on it. Then Graham, the Fat Duck's sous chef, appeared and thumbed a few sweets before leading us over the road to the prep room, which would be our prison for the next few weeks.

It was 100 yards or so away from the restaurant, in an old building perched on the side of a car park. Blumenthal's laboratory was on the top floor. I looked up at the window and wondered what sorcery was going on up there, and for some reason thought of the Soup Dragon in The Clangers. But there were no tours of the lab to be had, or soup for that matter, and they quickly got us to work.

173

A 23-year-old chef called Laurent ran the prep room. At first I thought he was French – he had that peculiar blend of Gallic arrogance and nonchalance – but it turned out he was Dutch.

He told me to measure out the venison and frankincense tea into exact 65g portions. It was probably the easiest job in the kitchen, but I managed to mess it up. I had to pour the broth into small plastic bags and vac-pack them. But a couple of bags exploded, and each time I had to clean the vacuum packing machine down and start again. I could see the sideways glances. They could tell I was a novice straight away – it wasn't just the Tesco bag and my two knives that gave me away.

I spent the rest of the morning prepping asparagus spears for the 'salmon poached in liquorice gel' dish on the taster menu. Each spear had to be perfect, like everything else in the restaurant. You cut a circle just below the bud, and peeled the stalk into a slender white arrow. Eighty were needed for each service, and the amount of waste was shocking. Handfuls of perfectly good trimmings, glistening like slimy, green tagliatelle, were thrown in the bin. It felt criminal throwing so much good food away.

And so much for that celebrity chef guff about seasonality and local produce. It was March, and the asparagus was flown in from Peru. But it was hard to knock Blumenthal for food miles when some of his customers flew thousands of miles just to eat there. Some of them probably had carbon footprints bigger than Wales.

AS THE hours went by, the jobs kept rotating and quickly became brain-numbingly dull. One minute we'd be slicing exquisite Joselito ham into julienne strips for the snail porridge, the next we'd be cutting onions and other veg on the slicer. It reminded me of factory lines I'd worked on as a student, injecting donuts with jam. To pass the time, I'd sometimes inject two squirts of the gun instead of one, and imagine the jammy explosions as people bit into them. It was the sort of humdrum work that I'd always promised myself I'd never do again.

We stood there four to a bench, peeling and chopping, and making banal conversation. Like most kitchens, the place was predominantly male. There were only four female chefs at the Fat Duck – and three of them were doing stages.

Claudia, a gnomish girl from Germany, had just finished a stint at the Gleneagles Hotel in Scotland. She told us how the G8 summit leaders had stayed there, and how they'd had to cook as FBI agents looked on. The publicity from the world's media was so good, she said, the place was packed out even in January. She gushed about head chef Andrew Fairlie's signature dish of home-smoked lobster with herb and lime butter sauce, and described how the shells were smoked over chips from old whisky barrels.

There was also a shy Irish woman called Jo, who barely said a word the whole time I was there. And then there was Martha, a 21-year-old giant who had just graduated from the Culinary Institute of America. Her only professional kitchen experience was three months part-time in a restaurant in Wisconsin. After another two months at the Fat Duck, she was going to spend the summer as a personal chef for a retired couple in the States. She was clumsy and loud, with no notion of personal space, and grabbed everything like a gorilla in a cake shop.

"I'm competitive," she'd say if anyone complained.

More than once I narrowly avoided losing the tips of my fingers as she blundered around the kitchen. She talked about her family incessantly, and as the hours ticked by, repeated the same stories.

The only paid female chef there was Laura, who ran the pastry section in the prep room. She was tough and fierce, and her pace never slackened. Laura was so fanatical about cooking, she would spend her precious days off eating in Michelin-starred restaurants to pick up tips.

At exactly 11am every day, we were led over the road for staff lunch. It was always a manic affair. Trays of food were lined up near the pass, and a haphazard queue formed as waiters and chefs jostled for position. We ate in the dining room, pushing each chair as far away from the set tables as we could. It did nothing for my digestion. Glass and the threat of admonishment sparkled over the napkins.

Less than an hour later, the wealthy and famous would start filling the same posh leather seats with no inkling that some sweaty-arsed chef had just been sitting there. Waiters skulked in dark corners as we ate, watching every forkful and speck of spittle.

One day, without thinking, I put a clean fork on the table and was screamed at from across the room. It was one of the big French cheeses. And he wasn't happy. "Don't put your fork on there!" he shrieked.

Laura hissed: "You're supposed to get as far away from the table as you can – turn the chair outwards!"

There were two meals a day – lunch at 11am and supper at 6pm. They were the only times we could rest our feet. And for five minutes we gobbled down our food, heads down and little talking.

The rest of the time we stood in the prep room, occasionally ferrying large plastic boxes of prepped food to the kitchen. They didn't seem heavy at first, but you had to walk slowly with your arms outstretched to prevent spillage, and then wait for a gap in the traffic as you crossed the blind bend.

And just when you thought your arms were about to give way, the worst bit came - weaving your way through the dining room. The fear of dropping two gallons of turbot stock over the carpet with an hour before service was terrifying. The waiters made it worse - it was almost like they were willing you to do it. Eventually, at collapsing point, you'd dodge your way through the chefs in the submarine kitchen, your arms burning with panic and fatigue.

Then it was best to get out as quickly as possible. If you stayed too long, a chef would collar you and get you to carry another box back to the prep room. If your timing was out, you could be yo-yoing back and forth, taking your life in your hands every time you walked through the dining room.

But the task I began to dread the most was the grapefruits. Even the chefs at the Hinds Head, Blumenthal's pub next door, knew about the grapefruits. The chore summed up everything you needed to know about the fastidiousness and downright ludicrousness of three-star Michelin cooking.

You had to carefully peel each grapefruit, without bruising or cutting the flesh. I was easily the worst, and more often than not I'd make a gash, and pink watery juice would ooze like an open sore. Then even more carefully, you'd take the white pithy globe and tease it into segments. Then with a paring knife, you'd pick out any pips and carefully peel away the white, and lay the pink flesh on towelling paper to soak up the juice.

Then the real work began. You picked each segment, flicking off tiny, juice-filled pearls on to another piece of towelling. The work was fiddly in the extreme. Even the slightest pressure would burst them. Once we had covered one piece of towelling with grapefruit pearls, we'd begin on another.

After an hour, your fingers were numb with the detail, and the urge to scream and hurl a grapefruit across the room was overwhelming. Some chefs used a toothpick to pick the pearls, but there was no easy way of doing it. Four whole grapefruits had to be picked for lunch and another four for the evening.

They were used as a garnish for the salmon poached in liquorice gel – barely making up more than 2% of the dish - and I hated every second of it. If this was cooking, then I was in the wrong game. I began wondering whether Blumenthal lay in bed at night devising ever more devilish recipes for his chefs to cook.

THE DAYS quickly became the same. We'd start work at 8am, and if we were lucky got away by 10pm. A 14-hour day with no pay, and little time to rest or slope off for a cigarette. If you were ever spotted standing idle for more than a few seconds, another job was thrown at you.

"We must push on," Laurent would say, whenever the pace slackened.

The only easy way to have a smoke was to bolt your food and light-up while the others finished their meals. Smoking was frowned upon – and I hid away near the bins at the far end of the garden. Only the waiters were quite brazen about it.

Once when one of the senior pastry chefs was puffing away a minute after staff lunch had finished, Jocky poked his head out of the back door and shouted: "Who the fuck do you think you are, Marco Pierre White?"

Laurent ticked off the jobs on his prep sheet as we did them. The potatoes for the lamb hot pot had to be cut on the slicer to ensure they were all the same thickness before you gouged out hundreds of walnut-sized discs. The off-cuts looked like hunks of Emmental cheese. Barely half the potato was used.

For the baby turnips, you trimmed the green stalk, and then scored a circle around the top before slicing off the root and scraping off the first layer of skin. Once you had a shiny, white moon, you shaved it until it was perfectly smooth, then vac-packed it in a water-filled bag for service.

The savoy cabbage was sliced into uniform strips. You pulled off the outer layers of the cabbage until you had the right shade of green, and then used the middle leaves, chucking away the inner-head because it was too yellow. Once you had a pile of usable leaves, you cut out the stalk, and sliced each side of the leaf into rectangles, and then into strips. Scarcely a quarter of the vegetable was used.

At one point, I was told to prep 5kg of tomato concasse, skinning and deseeding, and cutting the flesh into tiny squares. I've no idea how long it took me. Mid-way through, I asked Laurent what they were for, and he shrugged. All he knew was they were on the prep sheet, and needed doing. A few minutes later, I heard him on the phone to the kitchen. They didn't know either. Was that Blumenthal and his dastardly chores again? I imagined him upstairs in the lab, quaffing a red bubbling potion and laughing maniacally like an evil genius.

LAURA HAD an accident on her scooter so Jocky covered for her for a few days.

"It's a bit fucking quiet in here, isn't it!" he yelled, bursting into the prep room.

It quickly turned into the Jocky Show as he held court, yelling in the corner. His personality seemed to fill every crevice. He was like a crazed Highland imp gesticulating madly as he made his sardine on toast sorbet using brown bread and tinned sardines from Waitrose. The rest of the stagiers stared in awe, and Jocky was more than happy to answer questions.

When one of them asked how long he'd been at the Fat Duck, he said: "Four years and three months...and 17 days."

He was continually on the war path about whether anyone had made coffee, and if so, why he didn't have one. Because of his mad laughter, it was hard to know whether he was joking or not, and no-one dared find out.

The lab monkeys offered the only comical respite from the drudgery. They were a pair of goofy American chefs straight out of a slackers' movie. They would wander down the stairs from time to time to vac-pack their latest invention.

They were working on perfecting the ultimate banger – for Blumenthal's In Search Of Perfection programme - experimenting with the right mix of pork cuts, treacle, nutmeg and other spices, and recording each ingredient on a huge grid in the laboratory until they got it right. But they'd taken a break from the sausages, to tinker with the complexities of aerated chocolate eggs flavoured with mandarin oil. And like everything they did, they let us know all about it.

"You know, like, maybe we should make a sacrifice to the God of Aero or something," one of them laughed as they strolled in one morning.

"Yeah, maybe we could use one of these guys..."

They hadn't seen Jocky.

"Hey, what's going on in the laaa-aa-b?" he yelled, looking up from his orange and beetroot jellies (two small, square jellies are served on a plate - the reversal 'trick' played on the customer is that the yellow one is made from yellow beetroot, and the purple one from blood orange.)

One of the dudes mumbled on in a slow drone, explaining how they were having trouble with the mix.

"You know what chocolate's like," he drawled, "you gotta watch the viscosity."

180

At exactly 10.58am, Jocky started bellowing orders.

"Come on what the fuck you doing? Clean down! We're going across. Laurent – get them to fucking clean down!"

We carried that morning's prep across the road and tucked into sausage meat pie with beans and mash. At 6pm we went across for chicken with curried cauliflower. Then we spent the night pulling the guts out of pigeons.

We had a production line going with Laurent hacking away with a machete, fast enough to keep four of us going. We pulled out the guts, trying not to get blood on the skin. Then with the bird flat-side upwards, we prised the lungs from the rib cage, so they draped down like fallen red flags, and then ripped them out. Laurent said the pigeons would be hung for a week in the chiller.

"So it's very important to remove the lungs - they are the first to go off...they taint the meat," he added.

At 9pm, we had everything crossed off on the prep sheet, and were hoping for an early night, but Jocky had other plans. The ant man had come round the day before, but still they were scurrying around in the dry-store. I even found one on the main counter in the prep room. It gave Jocky the excuse to send us on a manic cleaning session.

"No wonder, we're getting fucking ants," he said, "who the fuck was the last to use that slicer!"

He started re-organising the kitchen, pulling apart cupboards, and ordering us to deep clean the place from top to bottom. Without warning, he'd launch a series of mock punches at Laurent, then stare around the room, barking orders.

At one point he spotted me loitering in a corner, my feet aching from all the standing. "Hey big man," he said, "I want

181

to see bubbles on both sides of that door!" The door wasn't even in the kitchen.

He then suggested a relocation of all the heavy machinery in the prep house, as Laurent looked on in horror. But after 30 minutes the dough mixer and slicing machine were put back in their original positions. But undefeated, he cleared an area near the walk-in chiller and shouted for everyone to pass him their knife rolls and boxes.

"See! We can put them here, for fuck's sake Laurent," he shouted. "It clears that space near the juicer and microwave..."

He was obsessed with space, but it was no wonder working in that stifling phonebox across the road year after year. Laurent raised his eyes, and looked like he was praying silently, as we handed over our gear. I had ditched my Tesco bag, and bought a cheap plastic toolbox for my two knives, and when Jocky saw it he was delighted.

"What the fuck's that! Jesus! You going fishing or something, big boy?"

We didn't get out until 11pm. I drove home and fell into bed after downing a couple of beers, knowing I'd have to be up in seven hours' time, shaved and showered. I looked at my red-raw hands and began to panic. The sleep deprivation and tiredness were already doing strange things to my head.

I wasn't being helped by the phone in the prep room either. There was no ring tone, and instead a blinding UV light would flash whenever it rang. After a while, with the sunlight streaming through cracks in the blind, and already light-headed from hours of work, it was hard to know if I was just seeing things.

It added to the headaches I was getting from the Snus (small bags of tobacco that you put under your lip) one of the Swedish chefs had given me. They certainly helped my cigarette cravings, and acted as a mild stimulant, but they gave me a pounding migraine.

I had a couple more beers, but still couldn't sleep. I then made the fatal mistake of looking at my alarm clock. It was 5.48am. The panic took over. I had an hour's sleep at most. Then I remembered they'd changed my rota and I was working in the main kitchen on the amuse bouche section, which meant I had to be in at 7.30am. Normally it was the one golden day a week for the stagiers, when they'd get a break from the prep room and see how it was really done. But all I could think about was losing that half an hour.

I got up, had a shower, and sat there drinking coffee trying not to think about the 17-hour shift in front of me. I was a cack-handed fool compared to the rest of the stagiers, let alone the paid chefs in the kitchen, and expected to last all of five minutes.

I got in at a minute past 7.30am and was introduced to a Canadian chef called Jon, who ran the amuse bouche section - a tiny area of the kitchen no bigger than a coffin. Jon was tall and wiry with greying hair, and at 34 the oldest chef in the kitchen by a few years, and younger than me by seven.

He explained that our section was responsible for four of the 14 courses on the tasting menu: oyster in passion fruit jelly with horseradish cream and lavender; pommery grain mustard ice cream with red cabbage gazpacho; jelly of quail with langoustine cream and parfait of foie gras; and sardine on toast sorbet with ballotine of mackerel 'invertebrate' and marinated daikon. And we also had one a la carte starter to take care of - radish ravioli of oyster with goat's cheese and truffle with rissole of fromage de tete.

I couldn't have wished for a better teacher. He was intelligent, mild-mannered, thoughtful, and if he was stressed, he didn't

183

show it – even when he had to chuck away my botched cucumber brunoise garnish for the gazpacho dish.

"They have to be squares, not flattened," he whispered. "But don't worry - we'll do them later."

As any cook will tell you, everything in a kitchen is overheard, even your thoughts, and a few seconds later Jocky came over and pretended to be busy at the sink. He gleefully examined my ham-fisted work, poking the little cubes with a spiteful finger, and smirking at his adoring pastry posse.

I knew they saw me as an imposter. I undoubtedly wasn't one of them. It wasn't just my knife skills. I just didn't tackle the jobs with the same insane energy. I'd always thought of myself as a passionate cook, but compared to them it was a passing whim at best.

I realised how big the chasm was when one of them joked about Blumenthal's obsession with food. They said that he used to go home after service, switch on his computer, and spend hours on internet forums discussing cheffing techniques. Perhaps that was what you needed to do to become the best? All I knew was that Michelin-starred cooking wasn't for me. They say the catering industry caters for everyone. But the way I was feeling about it, I'd have been happier running a whelk stall in Bognor Regis. At least I'd be getting some fresh air and a glimpse of the sea, and the nearest mad Scot could be bought off with a can of cider.

My first job was opening the oysters. They were gnarled, flat native types from Colchester and refused to give up their meat easily. I thought it would be a breeze, and hoped I might be of some use. But any delusions of being a decent shucker were soon dashed.

Normally I'd just stick the knife into the hinge, wiggle away, and with a flick of the wrist pop them open. But I hadn't encountered brutes like those before. I began to wonder whether they picked the native type because of their expense - or just because they were difficult to open.

I remembered a quote by Saki which goes something like: "There's nothing in Christianity or Buddhism that quite matches the sympathetic unselfishness of an oyster." But what the hell did he know? It was obvious he'd never worked in a kitchen. I prised and chipped away. It was like trying to engrave a gravestone with a lolly stick. After an hour, I had stab wounds in my left palm where the blade had sprung free. On my right, there were three ugly blisters, exposing large circles of red flesh.

Sea water and shell shrapnel were splattered over my board, and I had to wrap my hands in blue kitchen paper to cushion the wounds. At least sea water was good for cuts, I thought. But I must have looked an idiot standing there with my hands bound up like a blue mummy.

Occasionally, Jon would wade in and open a few, glancing at the clock. It was obvious we were behind, but still his patience and good humour continued. I was embarrassed at my cack-handedness, and fuming inside. But the more I stressed, the harder they were to open.

Maybe they could sense it? Maybe there was something in that saying: "The oyster is a gentle thing and will not come unless you sing." The mood I was in, I felt like throwing them in a strobe-lit cell and blasting Metallica at them at full volume.

As I worked, I thought about the time I'd queued up at an oyster hut in Colchester and saw a young lad popping natives effortlessly with a pen-knife. He did one every few seconds. I told Jon the tale, and he looked round at the mess on my board and my rags.

185

"Maybe we should get him in here," he said.

There wasn't even the slightest bit of sarcasm in his voice. Or at least none that I could detect. But then the sleep deprivation was doing funny things to my head, and I could barely remember my own name.

When the oysters were finally all open, I washed them twice in their sieved liquor to remove any shell shrapnel and drained them in a chinoise. Jon told me to lay the oysters on a board and slice them in half before pushing the meat back together.

You then put oyster shells on a tray, and squeeze a small slug of horseradish cream into each. You place an oyster on top, trying to match the largest with the biggest shells, and spoon passion fruit jelly over the meat to form a coating that sets in the fridge.

For service, you line up 40 slate blocks, and mix rock salt with egg white to form a salt ring on one end of the slate. You then wedge a stick of lavender into the salt, flat against the slate. You nestle a shell on the salt, and garnish it with two lavender seeds – one on each half of the oyster meat. You then stick a shard of pepper tuile into each half, and carry the dishes out to a table in front of the pass, where they are invariably scrutinised by a succession of waiters.

I was given one of the oyster dishes to try, and although I thought the combination of the flavours sounded odd, I was surprised by the taste. Each ingredient stood out, and you could still taste the oyster – but I didn't "get" the dish.

Blumenthal took scientific precision so seriously, his chefs used a refractometer (an instrument used by wine makers) to measure the sweetness of the passion fruit to get the 'perfect' combination of salt and sugar. Too sweet, for instance, and it apparently became a dessert.

But why passion fruit with oyster anyway? I read in one interview that he said it was "simply an inspiration". Yet there was nothing simple about any of his dishes. He has been described as either one of the world's most gifted, innovative chefs, or the greatest confidence trickster of his generation. And after eating that oyster, I was left with the impression that he could easily be both.

One thing stuck in my mind, and that was an interview with Ferran Adria, head chef of El Bulli, near Barcelona – a place Blumenthal denies he imitated, even if they do both serve outlandish molecular gastronomy combinations: Adria's oysters, for instance, are served in an essence of liquefied smaller oysters, with lemon relish, yoghurt and macadamia nuts.

Away from the mad science of El Bulli, Adria, often described as the world's best chef, said his favourite eatery was a tin-shack, family-run, 20-seater in nearby Roses. He liked to sit there scoffing boiled shrimps straight from the sea – no colorants, gelling agents, emulsifiers, acidifiers and taste enhancers, just the freshest seafood it is possible to eat, cooked lovingly with sea salt and olive oil.

And that image is something that has always intrigued me. The world's best restaurant doesn't necessarily mean the world's most delicious food. In fact, a (household name deleted) restaurant reviewer, who has eaten in all of the top restaurants in the world, once told me the best meal she'd ever had was a breakfast of fried monkfish and tinned tomatoes cooked by a fishmonger in Billingsgate Market.

And that was the way I felt about it all, as I stood frozen to my work station, with the constant call of "Backs!" behind me, my mind whirling with tiredness and still 15 hours to go. If it had been up to me, I'd have just wanted those delicious native oysters straight from the shell. No lemon, no Tabasco, no shallot vinegar, and certainly no passion fruit or horseradish,

187

just the flavours of the ocean and the ancient, fossily taste of zinc. But then, I suppose you can't charge a fortune for food like that.

For me, Blumenthal's cooking was not so much gilding the lily as turning it into a Baroque painting. And I hadn't even got on to the sardine on toast sorbet with the pretentious-sounding 'ballotine of mackerel invertebrate'. Oh, and don't forget the marinated daikon. It was nothing without the daikon.

THE GASHES and blisters soon made it difficult to work, and I had shovels for hands at the best of times. The size of the amuse bouche fridge didn't help much either. Each side was barely two feet wide, so you had to perform bizarre contortions with the trays of prepped food to have any chance of getting them in or out. The thought of seeing it all slide off the tray and crash onto the floor was terrifying.

I knew how precious it all was, because whenever we were asked to carry a container of sauce or stock across the road, Tom the saucier would be hot on our heels, pleading: "Please don't drop it - there's a week's work in there!" He almost had tears in his eyes at the thought.

To make matters worse, the quail jelly with langoustine cream and parfait of foie gras dish was served in a tilted cup. You carefully spooned pea puree in the bottom and covered it with warmed quail jelly, which set in the fridge. You then carefully spooned langoustine cream over the quail jelly, rolling the cup to make sure the jelly was covered before the cream set.

I'd made the basics for the cream in the prep room the day before by crushing langoustine claws in a huge metal dough mixer, and chopping up veg for the mirepoix. But of course I didn't actually get to cook it - like everything in the prep room, that was as far as your input went. And like all recipes at the Fat Duck, it was closely guarded and meticulously detailed. All I knew was you fried the claws with shallots, and then added cream, carrot, celery, sliced baby onions, white peppercorns and other spices before simmering it and passing it through muslin. But there were no doubt dozens more stages involved.

The dish was topped with a quenelle of foie gras and chicken liver parfait. After seeing I could barely open oysters, Jon was taking no chances with the quenelles, and it was at this point that I realised just how skilful three-star chefs are.

There was no two-spoon action as you see in most kitchens - Jon could make them one-handed in a second. A flash of a teaspoon, and there was a perfect brown egg. He rubbed the base of the spoon on his left palm to warm the metal and free the egg, and nestled the quenelles on a clingfilm-covered tray before seasoning them with salt, ground black pepper and a sprinkling of ludicrously finely-cut chives, which I hadn't cut either.

For service, a quenelle was carefully placed in the centre of the langoustine cream. I'd take each order out to the waiters and put them on the relevant silver tray before handing over the ticket. Sometimes, I'd pick the wrong tray, and the waiters would sigh and no doubt wish me an excruciatingly painful death.

Jon said very little as we worked. The only time he got excited was when he told me how a table of five had come in the day before, and spent £7,000 – a third of what the average British chef makes in a year. He seemed very impressed.

"The 12.5% service charge alone was more than the average bill here," he said. "But they weren't idiots though. They knew their food and appreciated everything…"

There were some idiots in for lunch that day though, as one of the waiters made clear as he bitched about them in the kitchen.

Two TVs in the kitchen allowed the chefs to see which table was about to clear. It had cost thousands installing the hidden cameras, and I wondered what the customers would think if they knew their every bite and slurp was captured on film.

"Look at that bastard on table 33," the waiter said. "He keeps going out every ten minutes, probably to put some powder up his nose. And look at the prostitutes he's with! It's disgusting!"

The pastry section gathered round to watch a coke-bloated man with highlighted hair texting on his phone. His skin was such a fake berry-brown, he looked like he'd been grabbed by the heels and dunked in wood varnish.

Next to him sat a pretty blonde and brunette, both in their early 20s. The women giggled as he continued to check his messages. None of them seemed remotely interested in the food. It was like feeding strawberries to donkeys. I thought about how much blood, sweat and science had gone into those dishes, but I couldn't help thinking the joke was on us. It was just food after all, and they were just customers. It was up to them how they spent his money.

The waiter came back minutes later to vent more spleen.

"Can we get a close-up of the blonde," one of the chefs joked. "If they're whores let's get their fucking number, you know what I mean!"

The manager disappeared tutting. "They're fucking peasants," he said.

Next on the tasting menu came the snail porridge, an amazingly vibrant dish as green as leprechaun's piss. The oats were cooked in parsley butter, and topped with snails from a farm in England. The garnish was julienne strips of Joselito ham, and shaved fennel. Then after the roast foie gras with almond fluid gel, cherry and chamomile, it was back to our corner for the sardine on toast sorbet.

190

Jon showed me how to line the plates with strips of daikon, marinated in sesame oil and other secrets. You placed a slice of mackerel ballotine 'invertebrate' on the plate, silver skin side facing north. The fish had been filleted but not skinned, and cured in salt, coriander seeds, lemon and lime zest. The fillets had been stuck back together using meat glue, and poached for a minute.

You then nestled a scoop of sardine sorbet – garnished with salmon eggs - on top of the daikon. The eggs were marinated for exactly 20 seconds in an equal mix of soy sauce and mirin before being drained in a tea strainer.

"Any more than that, and the skins of the eggs start to harden," said Jon.

As soon as the rush started, the buzz kicked in...

I couldn't believe I was doing service in the second best restaurant in the world. I was witnessing food history in the making. I was part of it. I was working in the gastronomic equivalent of the centre of the universe.

Alright, alright, there was the small matter that I wasn't actually getting paid, and to be fair should never have been let out of the prep room in the first place. But I had sole responsibility for the oysters, and my empire soon stretched to putting cucumber brunois in each soup bowl, and pouring the langoustine cream over the quail jelly. Jon did everything else, and I was still finding it hard keeping up with him. But as useless as I was, I could console myself that I wasn't being helped by the wounds on my battered hands.

Trying to pick up lavender seeds at speed with a battered thumb, and carefully placing them in juxtaposition on each oyster was hard enough. But cracking the tuile into decent-sized shards was even harder.

"You've got to be firm with it, just break it, you know what I mean," said Jon patiently as he balanced quenelles on six quail jellies, fried rissole of fromage de tete, and set out five sardine plates in the time I'd managed to pick up two lavender seeds.

A few minutes later we were really in the shit, and even Jon looked flustered. And then my suspicions about how useless I was were confirmed when he walked up to the head chef Ashley Palmer-Watts and whispered something in his ear. I could sense eyes on me, and a wave of paranoia hit me like bird shit on a windscreen.

I was already feeling anxious about one of the oyster dishes coming back. It had taken me so long to open them that I'd rushed the washing part, and kept thinking there might be an ugly time-bomb shard of death in one of them, ready to rip open the throat of a wealthy and highly litigious diner.

As each empty plate came back, my fear rose. Surely the odds on an oyster casualty were rising? I felt like a child with a peanut allergy being forced to play Russian roulette with a bag of Revels. I thought it through and wondered whether I would complain if I found a piece of shell in my oyster. Probably not. But then I wasn't a dreadful snob paying hundreds of pounds for a meal, or far worse, an amateur foodie. The only thought that consoled me was that it might be the berry-brown businessman.

Jon came back, and I tried everything in my power to pick up speed. But whenever I tried to cut a corner, he was on me like a hawk.

"No you want less cucumber in than that – the same as that one," he'd say as I waved a teaspoon over each bowl.

The standard couldn't drop for a second and that made me even more anxious about the oysters. I glanced round at the

TV screen, expecting to see a lady in a tiara clutching her throat, her face turning as blue as her blood.

The rush eventually subsided, but then came crashing back like a vicious tsunami. Seven a la carte orders came in for the radish ravioli of oyster with goat's cheese and truffle, and rissole of fromage de tete. Even I knew we were doomed.

The detail that went into them was frightening. It was the fiddliest job I have ever - or hope to ever - come across. The thought of my sausage fingers butchering those delicate fancies still gives me nightmares now.

The success of the dish rested on the thinness of the sliced radish, and Jon was taking no chances with that. He cut insect wing slivers with the finest setting on his mandoline, draped them on a piece of kitchen towling, then let me get on with it. He put a silver thimble on the plates where he wanted the ravioli built. It was right near the rim of the plate - that no-go area I'd always been told was 'waiter's territory'. But then nothing at the Fat Duck was conventional.

I set about the dish with a pair of tweezers, building the radish slices in a circle around the thimble, each overlapping slice meeting the middle of the previous one half-way. I took my time and tried to get it right, but my first two were rejected before I'd even completed the bottom ring. Yet even with my cack-handed efforts, I could see the kaleidoscope magic – it looked like someone had drawn Venn diagrams on a plate with a ridiculously thin pink pencil.

The fillings – a brunois of goats' cheese, black truffle and oyster - had already been weighed out like lumps of hash in clingfilm wraps. You formed it into a ball, placed it in the centre of the ring, then built up the radish wall around it. And with the clock ticking and the adrenaline pumping, I was soon shaking like a surgeon with a smack habit.

A minute later and the confirmation finally came: I wasn't a Michelin chef at all, and never would be. The nearest I'd get was four tyres and a road map. The whistle was blown, the red card was shown, and Claudia, helping out on pastry, was brought in to fill my place.

I was so daunted by the fiddliness of the task, I didn't even feel ashamed. The painful and simple truth was I wasn't up to it. I had tried my best and failed. I consoled myself that experience is simply the name we give to our mistakes, and no garden is without its weeds, and it's not failure if you enjoyed the process. But I'd hated every second of those raviolis.

I stood there for a moment looking round the kitchen, watching the white blur, and realising how alien it all was to me. I was like some wheezing Sunday league footballer, used to a can and a fag at half-time, doing a trial for Manchester United. I thought about that cup final at school when I'd been brought on late into the game and then substituted two minutes later.

I watched the head chef as he dressed each dish. He wasn't even looking as he administered the teardrop-shaped smears of sauce so loved in kitchens. His flourishes were so confident, so skilled. The pace didn't touch him. I tried not to think about the fact he was eight years younger than me, and even in another eight years I'd still be nowhere near his standard. This was a man at the very top of his game – and he stood there calmly at the pass, reading out orders and checking the dishes, and yet still gave himself time to take the piss out of the waiters. He was like a director staging a ballet in a broom cupboard, his chefs pirouetting away in that tiny space. But the thing that struck me most was how calm it was given the size of the kitchen and the complexity of the dishes. There was no shouting or raised voices, just calm, clinical execution.

I got a break from the kitchen when they handed me a tray of salmon pouches to vac-pack in Shed 3. Most of the meat and fish was cooked using the 'boil-in-the-bag' sous vide method (French for 'under vacuum'). The bags contained a perfectly square salmon fillet, coated in a liquorice gel which set at around 89C, meaning it stayed solid when gently poached in a digitally-set water bath.

The salmon was then removed from the bag and put on a plate garnished with grapefruit pearls, and two asparagus spears with coriander seeds balanced on them. It all appeared to be about small explosions of flavour from the coriander seeds to the grapefruit capsules to the lavender seeds on the oyster. I stood there lining up the bags in the machine, and gazing at the moon. I looked at its cracks and shadows. To be a top chef was all I'd ever wanted. I returned to the kitchen, and Claudia had finished the seven raviolis. Then the head chef called me over.

"How long have you been cooking for?" he asked.

"About a year properly," I said.

He gave a look of mild surprise – you can learn a lot in a year.

CHAPTER TEN

Somehow I got through the first week, and slept most of the Sunday and Monday. The alarm went off at 7am on the Tuesday morning, and it felt like I hadn't slept at all. I forced open the sarcophagus and got out of bed, struggling against the temptation of snuggling back under the sheets, and forgetting all about my insane idea of becoming a chef.

Working at the Fat Duck had only highlighted how much hard graft goes into Michelin-starred cooking. I wanted to be somewhere with a far simpler menu and less hours. Being on my feet 15-plus hours a day was soul-blanching tedium at best, however much I convinced myself that I loved cooking. The fact that I was both the oldest and worst chef in the kitchen made it all the more unbearable.

There was no doubt about it - those friends who had thought I was out of my mind for ever attempting to become a professional chef had been right all along. It was indeed a young man's game, and that became clearer every day as the pain in my feet, knees and back got worse. But something made me get up and face the long week ahead. It was not an in-built passion for the job - it was just I didn't know what else to do with my life. And I couldn't suffer the ridicule of going back to the paper. Not yet anyway.

I got in a few minutes late, worried about whether the clocks had gone back and I was actually an hour late. They all saw me glance at the prep room clock as I walked in. My first job was shifting the boxes of veg piled up outside the prep room door. Danny, the fat American, was in charge and slunk against the wall giving orders. Then he got us carrying stock across the road, tackling the fearsome assault course of vacuum cleaners, plastic bin bags and waiters.

We chatted to take our minds off the grapefruit, but none of the chefs had done much over the weekend – they were all too tired. I didn't tell them I'd spent mine with my hands smeared in manuka honey to help heal the oyster wounds.

Paul, as wild-eyed as ever, spotted them and said: "In some restaurants they'd rub lemons in your hands!"

"Why would they do that?" I asked, thinking for a second it was some sort of cheffing remedy.

He looked confused.

"They just would. Huh?"

He had an unnerving habit of talking all the time, and moved rapidly from subject to subject without any apparent logic. He would throw random questions at you, and finish each sentence with an immediate and slightly aggressive: "Huh?"

He had spent the first week charging about the kitchen, ploughing through each job maniacally. It was in direct contrast to my own waning enthusiasm. There had been several moments when I'd almost walked out. During one particularly low period, I voiced my frustrations as we carried stock across the road. I told him I was bored to tears and we were just grunts brought in to do the donkey work.

I'll never forget the expression on his face. As his loathing subsided, he told me we were here to learn, and it was a wonderful opportunity I was snubbing, and that I should be proud doing a stage at the second best restaurant in the world. The whole point of doing menial tasks, he said, was to get fast at them so you could move on to the more interesting stuff.

He stopped talking to me after that. Then the digs and rumours about me leaving began. He'd chide me endlessly about it over the chopping boards.

"You were about to quit last week, huh!"

"What?"

"You were about to quit, when we were doing the grapefruits. You were about to drop – I could see it in your eyes! Huh?"

"No, I wasn't!" I said, looking round to see if Laurent was listening.

"You were! I could see it. Huh?"

Later, I caught him bitching to the others.

"That's really bad, turning your nose up," he said as I walked in.

BUT AFTER a few more days in the prep room, even his attitude changed, and he stopped shouting "what's next?" so much. He even started talking to me again.

We were carrying stock across the blind bend, when he whispered: "I heard what you said last week. I heard you. This is donkey work, mate. It's alright for them young ones. But we're too long in the tooth for this. Huh?"

It was strange but his despondency seemed to boost my enthusiasm. Even more so when he told me he'd dropped a tray of quail jelly all over the amuse bouche fridge during the previous day's service. I was determined to finish the second week, maybe even do a third. But the idea of completing all six weeks of my stage was unthinkable.

I arrived the next morning, checked the rota, and found they'd put me down for service. I was surprised. After my last performance, I didn't think I'd get a second chance.

Then I looked at my hands. How the hell was I going to open 100 oysters? The manuka honey had helped a little, but the constant knife work had re-opened the wounds. A yellow crust had formed over two of them, which I presumed were the beginnings of scabs, but Martha had diagnosed - with a slightly pleased look on her face - as an infection.

I went over the road, and found a young American stagier called Eddy in my place. They were trying him out for commis, and Jon apologised and told me to come back at 4.30pm for evening service. He looked really anxious about telling me the news, but I can't tell you how relieved I was.

I went back into the prep room, and pushed 88 quails through the mincing machine for the quail jelly. I was told they didn't put the birds in whole because mincing increased the surface area, and therefore the flavour of the stock. I wasn't convinced. I was pretty sure you'd get a rich jelly out of 88 quails, regardless of whether they were minced or not, but what did I know? Again I imagined Blumenthal sitting behind a desk in his lab, stroking a white cat, and dreaming up dastardly new recipes to punish his slaves.

My fears were confirmed when I was told to finely cut 15kg of onions on the slicer. The dry-store soon became smoky with sulphur fumes, and an engineer fixing one of the ice cream machines next to me complained bitterly throughout.

"Jesus," he said, rubbing his eyes. "You need bloody goggles to work in here!"

I was suffering too, and although I'd read somewhere that chewing parsley helped lessen the effects of chopping onions, it didn't make a blind bit of difference. At least it would kill the ants, I thought. I returned to the prep room and cut 100g of celeriac into brunois. After a few minutes, Martha emerged from the dry-store, whispered something, and Laurent called me over.

"You didn't clean the slicer."

"I did!" I replied, outraged by the slight.

199

"You didn't clean the slicer," he repeated.

I went back and cleaned the slicer, which now had bits of carrot wedged behind the blade. Martha had obviously complained to Laurent, but it hadn't stopped her cutting her brunois.

I headed over the road in the afternoon, and got one of those rare moments of kitchen joy - Eddy had opened the 50 oysters I needed for evening service. My hands were saved, and I was able to concentrate on other jobs like juicing red cabbage for the gazpacho, and picking chervil leaves for the ice-filtered lamb jelly. Only the top piece of each chervil leaf was used. When the dish was served, they looked like tiny green footprints dotted over the lamb tongue, cucumber, and tomato confit garnish.

At one point, Danny squeezed past me to borrow a spatula from pastry. After a minute of whining, he stormed back into the main kitchen like a toddler refused sweets. I could hear him moaning to Palmer-Watts. He sounded like he was about to cry.

"Ash, can you tell the pastry section to lend me a spatula! They don't want to give it to me."

The head chef came through, listened to the arguments, and mediated calmly. He nodded a few times as the pastry posse went through an arraignment of unreturned items, and incidents when they'd been refused equipment.

"Guys, let's act like adults here," he said finally. "Come on - let's help each other out."

The pastry chefs then mimicked Danny's whining voice for the rest of service.

"Ash! Ash! Ash!" they giggled to each other, doing an impression of the barfly character in The Simpsons.

"Imagine if Jocky had been here," one of them muttered.

Evening service flashed by and I had no time to dwell on anything other than making everything as perfect as I could. Although no-one said anything, they seemed fairly pleased with my performance and I felt I had been of some use, even if most of it was just running to the sheds and back. They weren't going to give me a job, but the buzz had returned slightly and I remembered why I wanted to be a chef.

At one point, the head chef called me over to show me how to plate the turbot dish. It was stunning. It was topped with five pieces of sea urchin roe and came with langoustines and a turbot and verjus foam.

Although I wasn't too keen on the tasting menu, everything they gave me from the a la carte menu tasted of heaven. Sole veronique with pont-neuf potatoes; best end of lamb with onion and thyme puree and lamb shoulder, sweetbread and oyster hotpot; and pot roast best end of pork with truffled macaroni. But the best of the lot was the civet of venison. I'd never tasted a better dish.

Words were useless for moments like those, and I can't begin to describe the intensity of the flavour. It tasted ancient and magical, as though Herne the Hunter himself had galloped out of the nearby Windsor Great Park and dragged the blooded corpse of a stag through the restaurant. All it needed was an iPod playing the sound of hunting horns and baying hounds. I'm surprised Blumenthal hadn't thought of it.

With such incredible flavours in the meat dishes, I was beginning to see why it took a week to make a stock. Palmer-Watts said they rarely used bones, and nearly £200 of shoulder meat went into the lamb stock alone. The menu was beginning to look good value, given the labour and ingredients that went into it. But despite being full for months ahead,

201

there was no way they would have been able to turn a profit without the free labour.

THAT EVENING, I had a rare insight into the murky world of Michelin stars. I was cutting lavender stalks on a table in the garden when it happened. The head chef came out followed by the front-of-house team. Even the human resources woman was there.

He said a Michelin inspector had been round and given them feedback on an earlier visit. Palmer-Watts was upbeat, like a football manager drumming up morale at half-time, which was surprising given what he told them. The inspector had said the service started off well but slacked off during the evening. When he arrived, one of the staff had asked, "have you booked?" as though he'd just wandered in off the street. And to top it off, he then had to wait 25 minutes for his bill.

As for the food, the inspector was shown the kitchen and said it was even smaller than he'd heard. He was apparently amazed that such exquisite dishes managed to come out so rapidly from such a small kitchen. So much for service being more important than the food, I thought, but the Fat Duck still kept its three stars.

I drove back happy and exhausted. Seven hours later, I was back in the prep room, picking meat from confit pigeon legs for the pastillas. Laurent kept telling us to make sure we removed the sinews.

"It's not good for the customers to get them stuck in their teeth," he said.

As we stood there with surgical gloves on throwing pigeon meat into a plastic tub, Paul whispered to me that he'd had a word with Laurent, and told him there was no point in him just being there for donkey work. Paul was leaving the next day, and the news quickly spread round the kitchen.

I had no idea I was in any way implicated until I went across to the restaurant to pick up rhubarb ice cream and clarified butter during the lunch-time service. Usually you phoned for a waiter to take food across, but for some reason they asked me. Laurent looked me up and down, and said: "You look quite presentable."

Marco Pierre White was standing outside the restaurant smoking a Marlboro. I nodded at him and smiled, but he barely looked at me. So much for chef camaraderie, I thought. But then he hadn't been a proper chef for years, and nor had I.

I walked through the dining room, trying not to glance at the customers. The smell of expensive perfume was overpowering. One of the waiters scowled at me as I walked past the pass and picked up the ice cream. You had to carry everything in a Fat Duck gift bag, so the customers couldn't see it. The ice cream fitted in the bag, but it was impossible getting a big tub of clarified butter in as well. In the end, I wrapped it in a blue tea towel and was about to head back through when Jocky stopped me.

"How's Paul today?" he asked.

I began waffling for a bit, and he cut straight in.

"He's leaving isn't he?"

I feigned surprise, but Jocky was watching me closely, perhaps judging the level of mutiny in the slaves. I knew there'd been talk about me leaving as well. I mumbled something and hurried out. Marco was on his second cigarette.

Later, after we'd done the pastillas, Palmer-Watts made a rare visit to the prep room. He had a talk with Paul outside, but I caught the odd word through an open window. The head chef was obviously worried about losing free labour, and had arranged for him to spend the last three weeks of his stage at

203

the Hinds Head. I desperately wanted to escape the grapefruit too, and wished I'd said something first. But it was too late now, and I knew they wouldn't be too bothered about losing my cack-handed skills. Besides, two stagiers choosing a pub over a three-star restaurant would be an embarrassment.

I don't know why the Hinds Head seemed so appealing. Maybe because it was good, honest cooking? Maybe it was the chance to learn some long-forgotten British dishes like quaking pudding and mutton ham? But in truth, it was probably more about escaping the grapefruit.

I liked the fact Blumenthal had worked on the dishes with the food historians at Hampton Court Palace's Tudor kitchens. It reminded me of the time I'd gone there once to do some filming. We were recreating a Tudor banquet for the Discovery Channel. Apparently, American foodies loved all that - seeing the dishes Henry VIII gorged on.

The food historians showed us the amazing sugar work the Tudor chefs had spun for desserts, and how to make pork pies flavoured with rose water. But my favourite had been the tale of how the palace cooks roasted whole dolphins on spits. It was like something out of Porterhouse Blue. I don't know whether they were tuna-friendly.

There was something satisfying about going through those old archives and making dishes live again, and I wanted to see how they did it at the Hinds Head. I'd done enough fiddly prep work to know three-star cooking wasn't for me. I wanted nothing more than to run a pub somewhere, knocking out simple but delicious meals like rabbit pies and pheasant in cider. I wondered what Henry VIII would have made of snail porridge. He'd probably have declared war on France.

WE FINISHED the day doing one of the worst jobs on the prep list – cutting pistachio kernels in half. There were thousands of them, and even before we were a quarter-way through, I felt suicidal. Every time I looked at the bag it seemed to get bigger. It was soul-destroying work, but luckily one that only had to be done once a week or so.

The halved-kernels were caramelised and formed a garnish for the pigeon dish of poached breast pancetta, and pastilla of confit leg meat with cocoa and quatre-epices. There was a photo of the dish on the wall, and it showed the halved green kernels next to the pastilla – so much effort for such a small part of the meal.

"Why the hell do we have to cut them in half?" I whispered at one point, trying to stifle the urge to run to my car and drive off in a hail of gravel and forgotten tortures.

"Probably for the colour. Huh?" said Paul.

He'd perked up a bit. He was off to the Hinds Head the next day, and let us know all about it. He kept boasting about how he was going to learn the secrets of Blumenthal's famous oxtail and kidney pudding. He knew I liked pies.

A new stagier called Eric had joined that day, and looked incredulously at the ever-growing bag of pistachios in front of us. I could tell he was finding it as hard keeping it together as I was. Occasionally, he would let off near-silent sighs.

Eric worked as a private chef for Russian billionaires on yachts in Antibes in southern France. He was full of stories of diamonds and vicarious glamour. He talked endlessly about how rich his clients were, and it just made me feel more pitiful about my own existence.

I should have been the one lounging on yachts, drinking cocktails and munching lobster. And there I was, working for nothing; cutting mountains of pistachios in half for rich people to feast on.

I knew it was all supposed to be for something, so I could put 'Fat Duck-trained chef' on my CV (no-one would ever find out it had been mostly grunt work), but no restaurant of mine was ever going to use halved pistachios. Not unless Blumenthal was doing the chopping.

I tried veering Eric away from Ferraris and Zadora timepieces, and on to far less depressing subjects. But he'd be back on it whenever he could. In a bid to lighten the mood, I asked what the worst thing was they'd ever seen in a professional kitchen. Eric's story was by far the goriest. I doubt whether it was true, but he seemed sincere enough.

He said the incident happened when he was working part-time in a burger bar, getting himself through catering college...

"This dude came in for a job," Eric began. "He was about 17, and had never worked in a kitchen before, and they put him on the fryer. He was wearing this watch – I couldn't see what it was, but it looked more like one of those expensive German makes or something...

"And I said to him, 'Buddy, you wanna lose that watch, buddy you DON'T wanna wear that in the kitchen!' And he says something like, 'it was given to me by my grandfather'. And then half-way through service, guess what, the watch slips off into the hot fat...and without thinking he puts his arm in to get it out...It was like a reflex man!

"You could see the flesh disappearing on his arm like cooked ham. He said something like 'hey guys' and went down like a tonne of fucking mash! Man, that was gruesome! Worst thing I ever saw..."

That evening, the UV light flashed and Laurent answered the phone, looking round at the washing up piled in the sink.

"Smile please, customers!" he said quickly.

206

We had all of 30 seconds to clean up before a Spanish couple walked in followed by Palmer-Watts for a quick tour of the prep room. The couple owned the farm that supplied the Joselito ham, and stank of money - and this seemed to impress Eric immensely. They nodded their way around the room as the head chef gave a few introductions.

"And these are the stagiers. We have up to ten at one time, and they come from all over the world," he said.

It was clear from the way he said it, that we were like some strange race shipped over from the four corners of the earth, and seen as free labour. In an apparent slip of the tongue, Jocky had once referred to us as "slaves" during one of his whirlwind visits. "Remember we're not allowed to call them that," Laurent had corrected him quickly.

I STARTED enjoying the work more, and became more relaxed about the job. I had done every task on the prep sheet, and that gave me more confidence, and with the arrival of new stagiers I didn't feel quite so exposed.

One day I arrived and found I was the second one in the kitchen, rather than the tenth. I headed straight into the larder to slice celeriac and carrot into brunois, so I'd be busy when they handed out the grapefruit. Claudia was in there gathering parsnips to make her cereal flakes.

The parsnips were thinly sliced into coins, then dipped in stock syrup, drained, and dried. The cereal was served in a small green box with a tiny jug of milk on the tasting menu. The boxes were the size of those variety pack cereal boxes you got as a kid - the ones marketing people had cunningly devised so there was always an argument over who got the Coco Pops. Many of Blumenthal's dishes were about stirring childhood memories - the crackling space dust and so on.

Claudia looked shocked when I walked in. I looked round and then down at my whites.

"They'll look at you for not shaving," she said, brushing the growth on my face.

I remembered my hung-over decision not to bother shaving. Drinking before bed had become the norm. It was the only way to guarantee a few hours sleep otherwise I'd lie there, with the arches of my feet sending shock waves up my legs, and my back in constant agony. The bleariness from the booze also helped me get through the first few hours of chores. It seemed to turn the volume down a bit, and I quickly sweated it all out anyway.

"Maybe it's okay in here, in the prep room," she added, "but not over there. The chefs would be sacked for not shaving..."

I rubbed my chin. A slight paranoia rose inside me, and then relief. The truth was I was utterly exhausted and the thought of getting sacked filled me with no terror at all. I could already feel those soft, welcoming sheets against my skin.

No-one said anything about my stubble until we went over the road for sausages, bacon, black pudding, and all the trimmings. The chefs couldn't even leave a fry-up alone – the beefsteak tomatoes were stuffed with breadcrumbs and parmesan, and the scrambled eggs had industry-standard chopped chives in them. A weasely-looking French waiter was in the queue in front of me.

"You look at me strangely," he said.

His friend was tugging at his arm, but he ignored him. I don't know what I'd done to upset him. Maybe they'd had a complaint about the oysters after all.

"When is your birthday?" he asked.

"August. Why?"

He moved his head forward and studied my chin.

"Then I buy a razor for your birthday..."

I couldn't think of anything to say back. I was too busy fretting about that evening's meal. It was traditional for the stagiers to cook the staff meal on Saturday nights, and Paul had volunteered for the job, and quickly sucked me in as wingman for his "chicken vindaloo with all the trimmings". But he'd got out of it with his move to the Hinds Head, and the job had gone to me. Paul winked at me whenever he saw me after that. "Remember the staff meal," he kept saying.

The thought of cooking for three-star chefs filled me with dread, but if there was one thing I knew how to cook it was curry. Laurent looked concerned to start with, and suggested we bought in pre-cooked poppadoms to lessen the work load. But I quickly got on with it, chopping dozens of onions for the curry sauce. Laurent watched me for a bit and was soon sniggering away to a chef shucking scallops in the sink.

"He chops them brunoise," he laughed, eyeing my chunks of onion.

What is it with professional chefs? Why do they think everything has to be done by the book? It was a staff meal and I was cooking for 40 people with just one induction hob, and I was going to blitz the sauce anyway after I'd cooked the onions down with two massive tins of tomatoes. I made a great bowl of raita, and then poached the chicken in the sauce. I added more salt, a touch of vinegar and some ketchup and tried it again.

Graham, the sous chef, walked in to check on my progress. I had 20 minutes to go, but it had all been done. Why couldn't it be like that during service? I knew the answer – this was my type of cooking, and flouncing around peeling grapes wasn't. Graham stuck a spoon in and tried the sauce.

"That tastes pretty good actually," he said.

Pretty good! Praise indeed. Those evenings cooking curries when I lived above a kebab shop hadn't been wasted. And all I'd been given in the prep room was a packet of curry powder and a few spices. They all tucked in when it was served. Only the waiter who had chided me about not shaving was worried about breathing curry fumes over the customers. Even Paul said he liked it.

But despite my success, the meal turned out to be my swan song. I had the Sunday and Monday off and never went back. I made up an excuse about having flu, and after a couple of days they stopped calling. They were probably secretly pleased.

I LAY in bed for days, resting my muscles and trying to soothe my aching back, and reflecting on what I'd learned, and whether I still wanted to be a cook.

There is a huge difference between the glamorous lives of celebrity chefs we see on TV, and those that work in their kitchens. It is why there are so many people going into the trade. Once it was a job for youngsters who couldn't get into the Army or didn't know what else to do with their lives, but all that changed when the celebrity chef phenomenon started and reality shows like Masterchef started selling the myth that cooking leads to glitz and fame – rather than perpetual fatigue and long, unsociable hours.

I have heard tales of youngsters wanting to be cooks, because they can't be Premier League footballers or rock stars, and cheffing is the next best thing to be famous in. The reality is, of course, very different.

The chefs at the Fat Duck worked 16 or 17 hours a day, whereas I'd only seen Blumenthal once in the three weeks I worked there – and that was just for a few seconds. I knew he was there because of the gleaming BMW M5 parked among the sorry-looking collection of clapped-out cars and bicycles his chefs used to travel back and forth from their endless, arduous shifts.

Any hopes of the culinary genius coming in to shake our hands and thank us for working for nothing were soon dashed. The closest he got to the prep room was talking on his mobile on the stairs as he took a quick break from filming in the lab.

His human resources manager had explained to me when I started that the TV chef wouldn't actually be in the kitchen. He had a bad back, she said. I wondered how many of his chefs had similar ailments, given the long hours and daily gruel. I knew I had. But it got me thinking about whether he felt guilty knowing his old comrades were slaving away in his absence, as he swanned around on the rubber chicken circuit, travelling the world, and taking credit for their work.

It reminded me of that scene in Monty Python's Life Of Brian when the hapless terrorists - led by John Cleese's Reg (I'll call him Heston) – launch a raid on Pilate's palace...

VOICE-OVER: Heston, our glorious leader and founder of the FD, will be co-ordinating consultant, though he himself will not be taking part in any cheffing action, as he has a bad back.

BRIAN: Aren't you going to come with us?

HESTON: Solidarity, brother.

BRIAN: Oh, yes. Solidarity, Heston.

I've always thought there is something disingenuous about a celebrity chef who is never behind the stove – doing the thing he loves and made him famous. I had a whiff of it at Rick Stein's - but at least he had done his time, and was too old to absorb the daily strains of kitchen toil.

I knew the arguments from the 'so what?' brigade and the poison peddled by the PR people behind the chefs' brands. Their client had trained a skilled, loyal team who could run the restaurant in his absence so he could lounge around in TV green rooms, promoting his image, and ensuring a steady stream of bums on seats and more book sales. And, of course, the money was good – much better than running a restaurant anyway.

I'd also heard the argument from chest-puffing food critics if anyone questioned why the great chef was not actually cooking their meal himself: "You wouldn't expect Giorgio Armani to personally make your jeans would you!" And Marco Pierre White, Alain Ducasse, Gordon Ramsay, Rick Stein, Jamie Oliver, Heston Blumenthal et al were just brands after all.

But I had never quite understood the argument. Sure, Leonardo da Vinci might have had a team of skilled painters preparing his canvases, but he still turned up to add the odd brush-stroke.

I knew that in any creative process, there were always a few supernaturally-talented individuals who possessed a gift that can't be taught. It was that knowledge that propelled their restaurants to fame, and although it was possible to train up brilliant chefs to cover in their absence, they could not always mimic their talent entirely.

Motivation and the lack of personal recognition were strong factors alone, especially given the ludicrously long hours and the huge egos you find in kitchens. Does a ghost writer put the same amount of love into a book as a writer publishing under his own name?

And what about creativity? Faithfully churning out the same dishes year after year would surely be a killer for any restaurant. Where do the new dishes come from? Blumenthal had his lab, but that seemed more for his TV programmes. The Fat Duck menu had hardly changed in years, and he had only removed the oyster dish after they were blamed for the devastating norovirus outbreak that closed his restaurant for three weeks.

But more than anything, I just couldn't understand why they didn't just stay in the kitchen doing the job they were good at – however hard it was. In many cases, their egos had grown so large they saw cheffing as beneath them, and that seemed very sad somehow. When would the tired celebrity chef culture finally come to an end? When would the great cooks cook again?

As for the Fat Duck's dishes and other tasting menu-based restaurants like it, I began to wonder when people would get sick of alchemy, ingredient reversals, foam, cubism, and twee compositions like barberry bark infusions? Would theatrical tasting menus and molecular gastronomy one day prove to be as much of a derided fad as nouvelle cuisine? Or the one-time fashion for exotic meats like ostrich burgers and crocodile sausages – the latter a favourite with pub wags who liked to tell the waiter to "make it snappy". What would be next? Animal genitalia?

I was convinced that when the next new thing did come along, molecular gastronomy would just become another cast-off. A moth-eaten dress in a charity shop, gathering dust with retro kitchen gadgets like egg-slicers, melon-ballers, apple-corers, fondue sets and microwave omelette makers.

Indeed, how long would it be before every gadget-crazed foodie had a vac-pack machine or sous vide water bath tucked away at the back of the cupboard with the pasta machine and bread maker.

Fashions take time to die and become naff, of course, and I was sure versions of Blumenthal's boundary-stretching cooking would end up chalked on the specials board next to the pine and giant jenga.

Once-trendy favourites like braised lamb shanks, slow-roasted pork belly, and spice-infused sweets such as cardamom crème brulee or cumin parfait had become tiresome clichés. Would the TV wannabes start tinkering with ploughman's ice cream, pickled egg sorbet, or Marmite cheesecake?

Imagine the scene if they ever started serving up snail porridge knock-offs, or trout candyfloss at The Harvester...

"It's not bad Margaret, but I'm not raving."

"You should have had the nitro-builder's tea and black pudding mousse you had the last time, Bernard."

I had seen it already with cooks like Paul strolling around the Fat Duck with a notebook up his sleeve, badgering chefs for quantities and ingredients. And he was setting up a restaurant in northern Finland, of all places. Not that the Scandinavian contingent thought he'd have any success with a Fat Duck rip-off, trying to switch local tastes from steaks to pilchard ice cream.

But there were thousands more like him on stages all over the world, I thought, as I rubbed more Deep Heat into my back.

CHAPTER ELEVEN

I got a part-time job for £8 an hour at an Italian deli near London Bridge, making lasagne, melanzane parmigiana, soups, and tiramisu in the kitchen upstairs. We also did canapés and dinner parties. Some of the customers would bring in their own oven dishes so it looked like they'd cooked it themselves.

The hours were good – I only worked from 9am to 3pm, but I soon got bored with making endless gallons of Bolognese and white sauce, and chargrilling wheelbarrows of aubergines. Most evenings, I ran the larder section for a manic depressive head chef at a restaurant up the road.

But after a couple of months my savings ran out and the bank phoned to say they wouldn't extend my overdraft limit. There was nothing for it but to return to the paper. It was one of the hardest – and easiest – things I've ever done. My fellow hacks were delighted, of course, and ribbed me about "how the dream was over". They said it broke their hearts to see me eating canteen food every day. But one shift gave me the same amount of money I was getting in a week at the deli.

As the months went by, I kidded myself that I'd soon be back, maybe with my own restaurant or pub. But then they offered me a staff job with a good pension and decent health care, and I was too scared of the future not to take it.

I think the moment I finally lost faith in cooking for a living was when I put my back out lifting a stock pot at the deli, and had to spend my whole day's pay on a 30-minute physiotherapy session. The physio spent 10 minutes of it on the phone talking about an injured horse.

But I still couldn't escape the call of the onions. I only had to watch a Floyd re-run and it all seemed so possible again –

making a living from the thing I loved, being a bon viveur without a care in the world, unshackling myself from the mortgage and opening a little bistro banging out old fashioned classics from the attic. Coq au vin, cassoulet, venison stew with dumplings, razor shells like they cook them at La Boqueria fish market in Barcelona, pan-fried sole with caper sauce, and proper steak and kidney pudding.

I missed falling into bed with shattered limbs, and sleeping the sleep of the just. I missed working in a trade where talent was rewarded, and promotion came with hard work and talent rather than the ability to brown nose the boss. And I missed the creativity as well.

I'd got disillusioned at the Fat Duck, realising that the higher you got in the restaurant industry, the more it was about consistency, and the more it felt like you were working in a sausage factory. But there was still a skill to it. Far more than the cowardly new world of formulaic, Twitter-fed, desk-bound churnalism.

And I knew there would be far more creativity in running a bistro, thinking of new ways to use up kitchen scraps. And that to me had always been the truest and most worthwhile form of cooking: making ordinary ingredients taste good. Surely that was why soup was invented? And soup, for my money, was the best meal in the world.

When I returned to the paper a few of the hacks muttered: "Well, at least you've been learning something useful for the past two years, not like being stuck in here anyway." The others just thought I'd been to prison. And I had learned something. I was never going to be Marco Pierre White. But I could throw a decent dinner party, serve up a damned good steak, and run a section in a busy restaurant. In fact, I'd learned a huge amount in those two years, and I sorely regretted not trying harder.

216

I started writing a blog about my experiences working as a chef, and the more I remembered them, the more I missed professional cooking. I never did find that fisherman's shack I wanted to cook at, shucking scallops on the quayside, and haggling over crabs.

Instead I was paid to write tedious stories about the updates Paris Hilton sent to her Twitter followers, or hat-botherer Pete Doherty's latest antics. My knife skills were still passable even after a year back at the paper. But I had serious doubts about whether I'd be brave enough to throw it all in again. There were only so many times I could go back to journalism. I knew that if I left again, and it didn't work out, I'd probably find myself swigging cider with the bench boys.

I asked to go part-time, but they said no. I asked to go freelance again, but they said the new editor would see it as disloyal giving up a "good job" to become a shifter. The only way was to give it all up, and throw myself into cooking again.

I had dreams of going to California, where they deep-fried scallops, and served steaks so big they made your eyes bleed. I fancied learning Mexican dishes on a food truck in San Diego, or shucking oysters in San Francisco, or pan-frying veal in Vegas, or getting a private chef job for some Lala Land bigwig who was addicted to lobsters and truffles.

I kept thinking about the Canadian chef at the Fat Duck, who worked on billionaires' yachts in the Med. He had a happy life, even if he was woken up at 3am to make sandwiches for pissed Russians.

But then the fear and doubt would set in and I'd see it clearly and painfully for what it was – a middle-aged man giving up a reasonably well-paid job, with a good pension and decent health care, and a nine-day fortnight, for a job with long hours, bad pay, and absolutely no guarantee of success or happiness. But then there was the possibility that one day I'd be running my own business, maybe even that fish restaurant overlooking the sea.

I SETTLED for a compromise, and got a voluntary job cooking at a homeless centre in my spare time just to see if I still had the passion. There was a soup kitchen at the top of my road, and I figured they probably needed some help judging by the number of drunks and tramps who crowded the pavement every lunch-time.

I knew it would be far removed from proper cheffing, and I wasn't on some sort of Jamie Oliver crusade trying to get crack-heads to pluck fruit from bins rather than mauled fried chicken. I suppose I wanted to help others rather than just dwell on my own feelings and failings. Maybe it would make me feel better, knowing there were people far worse off?

I walked past the centre a few times, and then finally went in. I asked about a cooking job, and was told to meet Sister Harpiner at the foot of the stairs. She took me up to her dusty office, and I told her I'd worked in a few restaurants before and would love to help out in the kitchen.

"That's great, Lennie," she said. "But we don't want anyone too good...because the cook's...well, we don't want her to get used to having someone good around and get frustrated when you're not there."

"I'm not Gordon Ramsay," I blushed, suddenly aware that I'd probably already said too much.

"Compared to me you will be," she smiled.

I was told to return at 11am the next day. I was late, but it was obvious the whole place was run on chaos. I told them why I was there, and a small search party was sent out to find Sister Harpiner, bellowing at the foot of each flight of stairs. I was quickly going off the idea and kept eyeing the stairway down, but there was always a grey-haired helper behind me, ferreting in bin liners, and blocking off my escape.

After giving up the search at what felt like the tenth floor, I was taken down to the kitchen and introduced to the pot wash, a small, cheerful woman in her 50s. She introduced me to some of the workers, and then went back to her foam.

There was a great emphasis on staff tea and biscuits. Every time I held up a half-nibbled chocolate digestive in protest, they told me I was allowed two. Five biscuits later, I met the cook I'd be working for. She was a gnarled, unfriendly woman with bow legs and heavy make-up.

That day the homeless, as she called them, were having potato waffles, peas, and chicken nuggets. Looking at the Iceland bags piled up in the corner, there was nothing to suggest it was different from any other day.

The food was cooked two hours beforehand, and left to pant in silver trays. It reminded me of school meals. Where was Oliver when you needed him? But there was no point in his brand launching a homeless meals crusade because tramps don't own televisions. And no-one cares what tramps eat.

The cook scowled at me several times. Maybe she'd been warned I was some sort of hotshot chef? She mumbled a few words, and then looked across the kitchen and smiled slightly.

"You can open those if you like," she said, pointing to ten large tins of evaporated milk.

She showed me a hitlerite contraption that looked more like an instrument of torture than a tin opener. It had a massive spike that you slammed down into the top of each tin. She did the first two and then left me to it. I saw her smirking as I mangled the first one, then the second. I was looking around red-faced and about to ruin a third, when another helper rescued me.

"I did that to start with," she said.

She finished the rest of the tins, and they obviously thought I'd done enough work for the day because they sat me down next to a smartly-dressed pensioner, and gave me another biscuit. He was reading the sports pages, and began discussing last night's game.

"You can't sit back on 1-0 when they've got all those millions on the pitch!" he kept saying.

The others told me he could measure shirt collars on the clothes left outside the door just by glancing at them. He'd made his money as a tailor, and had decided to give something back by buying the building and turning it into a homeless centre, much to the annoyance of the well-heeled neighbours.

An hour later they found Sister Harpiner. She took me upstairs and gave me some forms to sign. Occasionally helpers would bustle in, saying they'd lost something, or where were the keys, or what room were the scarves in? She told me about the place, and was sniffy about its sister centre up the road.

"There, they just have a bit of tea and toast," she said.

"Here - they have a hot meal."

"Sets them up for the day, I suppose." I said.

"And so it does, yes. And do you know how easy it is to become homeless, Lennie? Some lose their jobs and end up on the streets. Some go into hospital because they have mental problems, and come out after a few months and haven't kept everything up to date, and have got behind with the rent, and before they know it, they're turfed out. Or others split up with their wives and lose the house, and end up on the streets that way..."

I wondered how many ended up there because they'd tried to make it as a professional chef in their middle years.

I went in the next day, and never bothered to go back. It was obvious the cook wasn't going to let me do anything. A few weeks later, I was walking past the centre, hoping no-one would see me, when I spotted Sister Harpiner getting out of a car. I hunched down, trying to shield my face with the cans I'd bought from the off licence.

"Oh, hello there," she called. "Will you not be coming to join us?"

She called out again, and I finally got the key into the lock. It sent a cold, worthless shiver down my spine, trying to give a nun the slip.

I WAS at work a few days later when a story broke on the wires, saying: "TV chef Keith Floyd has died. He was 65." It upset me deeply. My hero - the man who had made cooking acceptable, and inspired me to become a chef – had died of a heart attack at his friend Celia Martin's home in Bridport, Dorset.

I went back that night, bought two bottles of a red I knew he'd be proud of and stood in the kitchen toasting his memory. Then I started on the Johnnie Walker Green Label and raised more glasses to him.

Floyd was diagnosed with bowel cancer after setting up a restaurant on the Thai island of Phuket. The venture crashed, he was involved in an acrimonious divorce battle with his fourth wife, and he went back to his farmhouse in France, impoverished and worrying about whether he would even keep his beloved fishing rods.

A film crew visited him at his farmhouse and made a documentary about him a couple of months before he died. It had been on the previous night, and had been dreadful to watch. It turned out Floyd passed away as he sat down to watch it.

From the moment the great cook was shown sleeping on a hotel sofa like some befuddled Chelsea Pensioner, his energy and spirit finally succumbing to a lifetime of fags and booze, it was clear it was going to be uncomfortable viewing. It was like watching the last hours of a dying God.

I tried to switch over several times, but it was Keith Floyd...

He might pull through and show his old magic, even a glimmer of it would do, I thought, but by the end I felt overwhelmingly sad, and desperately so the next day when I was told he'd died.

I wanted him to remain in my thoughts as the skewed bow tie-wearing roué lambasting Clive the cameraman, glass in hand, pan-frying sweetbreads and truffles, and heartily recommending that half the bottle should go into the daube, and the other half into the cook.

I wanted to remember him in his prime, drunk on the riverbank, hurling stones at a hapless fisherman who'd failed to catch any trout for the show. I wanted to remember him in Padstow, pretending to forget Rick Stein's name as the fresh-faced cook squirmed on camera. I wanted to be reminded of him serving a breaded beermat to a customer who'd complained about his Wiener schnitzel, and the live cookery demonstration when he'd left the giblet bag inside a roast duck.

I didn't want to remember him as the frail, doddering, aged-beyond-his-years man in Channel 4's appalling documentary.

As I stood swaying in the kitchen, drinking to his memory, it made me realise just how much I'd miss his infectious love of food, and his humbleness and readiness to accept where he'd come from - unlike the celebrity chefs spawned from his success, who'd become absorbed by fame.

Unlike them, he was a man who had always remembered he was just a cook. And it also made me realise just how much I missed cooking, however bad the hours and fatigue. I drank more Scotch and put on a CD of his favourite band The Stranglers. Their song No More Heroes Anymore came on, and I wept for the first time in years.

I INTERVIEWED Martin for the paper, and she told me how she and Floyd had celebrated her 65th birthday with a lunch of oysters, potted shrimps and partridge at Mark Hix's restaurant in Lyme Regis, Dorset. It turned out to be his last gourmet meal. Floyd had always said he would choose oysters for his last meal.

That evening, he told her he hadn't felt better for months. She said she was still in shock from his death, and kept expecting him to walk into the room. She was still finding his cigarette ash around the house.

She told me he was to be cremated in a banana leaf coffin in Bristol, the city where he ran a string of restaurants and launched his cooking career. She'd chosen the coffin because of its environmentally-friendly nature, and partly as a humorous nod to his love of cooking with leaves.

"You don't think it's a bit sick do you?" she asked.

"No, I think he would have liked it," I replied.

I was sent down to cover his funeral, but it didn't get many column inches the next day, mainly because there were no celebrity chefs there – not even his good friends Marco Pierre White and Jean-Christophe Novelli.

Floyd's latest autobiography came out a couple of weeks later. It hammered home just what an amazing life he'd had, and all the gambles he'd taken, and made me realise that anything would be better than just counting down the years at the paper.

A COUPLE of months later, they started making big cuts at the paper, and I took voluntary redundancy. The pay-off wasn't huge, but it gave me the chance to cook again.

I worked for an agency cooking at restaurants in London. Then I spotted an advert for a film location catering firm knocking out grub for the new Bond movie. I loved the thought of cooking outside and the travel that might come with it. I phoned up and they gave me the job without an interview.

I arrived at the airfield at 2.30pm in the blistering heat and was directed to the far side of the site by security. No-one asked to see any ID. I pulled up at another cordon that said "film crew only" and they waved me through.

I spotted the catering trucks straight away, next to the smart, white trailers where the stars rested between takes. A number of chauffeur-driven limos were idling outside. The whole area was filled with security men and riggers in fluorescent jackets.

I was met by a wiry, olive-skinned man in his 50s called Mario. I was expecting chefs in whites and hats, but the dress code was informal to say the least - just jeans, T-shirts and striped aprons. I had my whites tucked under one arm. Mario saw them and tutted: "You won't need those – it's too hot for whites."

He lit a cigarette, inhaled deeply, and introduced me to the rest of the crew. There was a man in his early 30s called Dom and a swarthy Italian in a bandana making salads in one trailer. Next door, in the main kitchen, an ogre in a camouflage T-shirt was frying dozens of eggs. Behind him stood a tall man with a knife slash across his nose.

"I won't bother introducing you to them," said Mario.

"They are Czech and speak no English."

The ogre and his friend nodded as I walked through. Mario told me to set up my board on a plastic box outside, and cut boxes of cauliflowers into florets. I'd been working for a couple of minutes when he came back and said: "Leave that for the moment, you can help with the serving in the tent."

I was worried they'd seen my knife skills and had me down as a waiter. I left the florets baking in the sun with the other prepped veg and followed Mario into a huge marquee. There were food counters in one corner and I was told to work with a woman called Sarah. She was serving up plates of fried breakfast, and looked stressed and at the point of tears, but it was difficult to tell behind her sunglasses.

For the next hour I worked non-stop. The orders flew in as I threw fried eggs, bacon, burgers, sausages, chips, grilled tomatoes, mushrooms and beans on to paper plates. As each tray finished, I'd run to get more supplies from the ogre.

A lot of the crew asked for burnt bangers for some reason. "Not that I'm saying you burn your sausages," one of them said. I looked down at the pink bangers, and dug out the brownest ones from the bottom of the heap.

Eventually the queue died down, and we sat down and had our meal. The cooks said normally there were 300 crew to feed, but it had been much busier over the past few days because there were 150 extras on set. They told me about life on the road. A couple of them had been doing it for six years. Mario had been doing it for 20.

"Once you've done this, you'll never want to go back to a real kitchen," Dom said.

The talk was all about sex and locations they'd worked at. The Bond film had started in January and they'd spent the last few months in Prague, Venice, and The Bahamas. Sometimes they'd get special requests from the stars – the actresses tended to want plain, boiled vegetables with no seasoning. But most of the time they just ate the same food as the crew. The latest Bond, Daniel Craig, often sat down with the riggers and stunt men, they said.

"He's really down to earth," gushed Sarah, "he even came on the chartered plane with us. He didn't want special treatment."

Mario got me to help him carry two huge beef joints from the refrigerated truck, and cut them into hundreds of steaks. I trimmed the fat and laid them on trays in the fridge ready for the evening meal.

The washing up was done under a gazebo behind the trucks. Two Poles washed the trays, plates and cutlery in massive tubs. One of them rinsed them down with a hosepipe, and then they were scrubbed in hot water and left to drain on picnic tables. They both worked with their tops off, and stopped for regular cigarette breaks and chatted in Polish constantly. Every time I brought more washing up, they would smile and say: "Oh, wonderful!"

I finished off the cauliflowers and cut up a sack of onions into julienne strips for hotdogs. It was fantastic working in the open air, and the sulphurous effects of the onions were blown away by the summer breeze.

Dom walked past at one point and said: "You can take your top off if you like."

I hesitated for a moment, and he pointed at one of the pot-bellied plongeurs and said: "You can't look any worse than he does!"

Mario took me into the main kitchen and got me to deep-fry batches of potatoes before finishing them off in the oven. The trailer was about 30ft long and as good as any restaurant kitchen I'd been in. In fact it was bigger and better set out than the Fat Duck's kitchen, but then we were catering for 400 not 40.

The crew were due to eat again at 8pm and Mario told me I'd be on steak duty. We made up a barbecue in a huge oil drum near the washing up area. At 7.50pm the coals were glowing nicely, and I'd lined up the steaks and salt and pepper ready for battle. But then a woman with a walkie-talkie wandered over with the bad news.

"They're not going to break until 9pm," she said snootily.

The kitchen crew scowled and put everything back in the ovens. They said sometimes the meal was put back four hours and it was a nightmare keeping food warm in the middle of a field. The coals were dying down, and I put some more charcoal on. Five minutes later the runner returned and said they would break at 8pm after all.

The place turned into chaos, and I frantically tried to fan the flames to get the coals going.

"Cook them all blue to start with and then finish them off," Mario yelled at me from the kitchen.

The choice was turkey, fish or steak for the main, but of course they all wanted steak. I could only do about 20 at a time, and it was taking a good minute just to get one side brown. The grill wasn't even hot enough for singe-marks.

I filled a tray with the first batch – they were rare at best – but there was no time to wait and the waiters whisked them away before I could stop them. I'd just finished turning over another layer, when Dom came back yelling for more.

"Just give us what you've got!" he kept shouting.

But they were still raw, and I made excuses about the heat of the coals. Greg, the firm's director, rushed over, demanding steaks, and I made more excuses. He ran into the kitchen yelling at Mario.

"You've got to keep a fucking eye on them," I could hear him shouting.

Greg ran off somewhere and Mario jumped out of the trailer and bollocked me for not putting more coals on. I fanned the flames frantically with one of the trays, hoping to build up heat. The steaks had barely seen the grill for a minute before they were snatched away. As soon as each side was sealed I chucked them in the tray. There was an inch of blood in the bottom.

Eventually the panic subsided and they stopped yelling for steaks and I could cook the last tray properly. Mario stuck his head out of the kitchen.

"I'm sorry you were in at the deep end," he said.

I shrugged and blamed the coals again.

"It's not that," he said, "it's those fuckers, fucking around with the time."

There was real hatred in his voice. Twenty years of it.

We started clearing down, and for the next two hours I helped with the washing up, trying to dry piles of plates and trays with paper towels. We worked under halogen lights and soon I could only see shadows. I was told it was going to be a long night because the shoot was moving to Pinewood the next day and we'd have to pack everything up and move before they got there.

228

At midnight, I was told to cook about three tonnes of bacon and sausages. They went in baguettes, wrapped in foil. Then at about 1am we laid trays of curry and rice, pasties, pies, baguettes and crisps on the floor of a coach and drove a mile to the end of the runway.

Even from a few hundred yards the flood-lit scene was dazzling. A Boeing 747 was surrounded by flashing blue lights from emergency service vehicles. Sam, one of the catering assistants, explained the scene: James Bond was fighting a baddy in an out-of-control truck careering towards the airliner, and some sort of military parade was taking place.

He had seconds to control the truck before it crashed into the jet and caused a massive explosion. She said it was supposed to be Miami airport.

"Have you got your passport?" I asked her.

"We don't need one – we're VIP!" she laughed.

She told me Richard Branson had flown in one of his Virgin planes to get it into the shot, but it had been heavily overcast and you couldn't see the Virgin logo.

We took a tray each and handed out food, napkins and plastic cutlery to the crew. The directors were sat in a covered area surrounded by editing equipment.

Suddenly a woman next to me bellowed "ROLLING!" and hundreds of extras ran about screaming as the truck careered towards the plane. They filmed the same scene five times, and then all the food was gone and we went round with packets of French Fries.

Sarah approached the film's director, a foppish-looking, grey-haired man wearing a baseball cap.

"Would you like some French Fries?" she asked.

"Don't be ridiculous," he said.

One of the extras had fallen over in the mayhem and was treated for cuts and grazes in one of the ambulances. About 30 minutes later, we climbed into the back of a pick-up truck and were driven back to the kitchen. Sarah said it was illegal to ride in the back of pick-ups on shoots, so we had to crouch with our heads down.

The rest of the team had gone without telling anyone. I left at 2.30am, at the end of a gruelling 12-hour day. It was harder than kitchen work somehow. There was far more running around and lifting, but you were out in the open air with the sun on your face, and I loved it.

Greg told me that the new Masterchef series was sending three contestants to work there for a day. It seemed strange that people would do that sort of back-breaking work for nothing. He said he'd start me off on £9 an hour and take it from there. He said the following week we'd be heading out to Jamaica, and told me to make sure my passport was up to date.

I went in the next day and cooked for three of the actors. They just wanted steamed vegetables. I served them with tamari and toasted sesame seeds and they asked if I did dinner parties.

For the first time in my cooking career, it really felt like something was happening. It wasn't haute cuisine, but Greg said you sometimes had to put on a spread. He said he'd catered for a film in Kenya, and at the end Angelina Jolie handed him $50,000 and told him to serve a thank you meal for the crew. She wanted lobster. He said it took him two days to arrange to get 500 lobsters and crates of champagne flown in from Mombasa. He said it had been a wonderful meal.

EPILOGUE

It was Christmas Day and the sun was beating down, but there was a refreshing breeze blowing across the white sand beach. Rick Stein was off in the distance shooting a scene with some Thai fishermen. They were showing him how to catch sting rays. I raked up the coals on the barbecue and threw another load of charcoal on the fire.

The sweat was pouring off my brow and I took another deep swig of my ice cold Chang beer and began prepping the squid, steak, and barracuda I'd bought from the market for our Christmas meal.

A whole suckling pig was roasting on a spit over slow-burning embers. I'd lined the inside of its stomach with turmeric, salt, and crushed black pepper and coriander root, and stuffed it with basil, lemon grass, mint, galangal and garlic. Then I'd basted the skin with lime juice and thick, rich soy sauce for colour and flavour. The smell was incredible.

A Thai chef called Tum was chopping away with a machete, making green papaya strips for our som tam salad. I threw green chillies, lime juice, garlic, fish sauce, dried shrimps, palm sugar, peanuts, green beans and tomatoes into a pestle and mortar and began bruising and crunching them for the rich vinaigrette sauce. Another gang of Thai kids descended and I tossed them more sweets.

"Thank you mister," they said as they scrambled in the sand.

I had far too much food for 20 crew, so I barbecued some squid for them. There were few finer pleasures in life than fresh seafood on the beach. Then the runner rang. The crew were about to break.

"Are you sure?"

"Yeah, I think they mean it this time," she said.

I raked up the coals again, and threw barracuda and catfish on the grill. The palm oil sizzled and soon an incredible smell of soy sauce and fresh chillies wafted out to sea. I opened another Chang and handed one to Tum.

His daughter was busy laying the tables. She arranged the salads, soft-boiled eggs, and sticky rice on banana leaves, and filled trimmed bamboo shoot utensils with sweet chilli sauce and fiery chilli paste. This would be a meal to remember.

I thought about my friends back home, waking up early in the freezing cold to put their turkeys in the oven. I wouldn't swap it for the world. Christmas on the beach, or cold and gloom in Blighty? It was a tough choice.

More kids descended and I gave them the last of the sweets. I looked over at the plush resorts surrounding Patong Beach. I could see the boutique hotel where Floyd had opened his restaurant.

I gazed up at the cheerful blue sky, and imagined him up there swigging large vodkas in a hammock. I hoped he could see me, and the happiness I'd finally achieved through cooking. I remembered the old Buddhist saying: "The love of work is the secret of success." And might I say it summed up my new life beautifully.

About the Author

Alex Watts is a travelling journalist and sometime chef, currently eating and writing his way around SE Asia. He has written for TV, radio and national newspapers in the UK, America and Australia. He also writes the blog Chef Sandwich - a journal of his food/travel writing.

Connect with me online:

Twitter: http://twitter.com/alexwatts

My blog: http://chefsandwich.blogspot.com

Lightning Source UK Ltd.
Milton Keynes UK
UKOW030633290312

189799UK00002B/5/P